THE UNLIKELY MASTERS OF ROCK

COMEDY

An origin story.

A therapy session.

A comedic roast.

EMERY

THE UNLIKELY MASTERS OF ROCK

Editor: Matt Johnson

Copy Editor: William Corbin

Cover Design & Layout: Caitlin Thompson

Book Design & Layout: Kane Killgore

Table of Contents

Prologue

1	EMERY???	1
2	SONS OF THE CONFEDERACY	13
3	ZOD, THE BENEVOLENT	27
4	COLLEGE BOYS	47
5	SETH THE ENTERTAINER	67
6	JOEY QUITS	89
7	THE GOLDEN CHILD	117
8	2,736 MILES FOR A DAMN STARBUCKS	127
9	A NIGHT WITH THE "THE SHAMAN"	145
10	THE WEAKS END	195
11	A FEW WORDS ON CHOPPER	208
12	DAVE POWELL	225
13	THE NAIL	237
14	MY BEST FRIEND, TOBY	251
15	ARE YOU STILL LISTENING?	269

Prologue

I'm fortunate to work with a publisher who allows me to make disclaimers. BC Words is owned by BadChristian, and BadChristian is owned by Matt Carter, Toby Morrell and Joey Svendsen. They are responsible for allowing me to write whatever I want; and in this particular instance I am writing about them. Matt and Toby are of course members of Emery and Joey was an "original" member before the band ever really got off the ground.

Much of the BC world operates on the grounds of transparency. That means, say whatever you think or feel, for better or worse. This philosophy does not come with the intent to cause problems or hurt others, but instead to just be your FUCKING SELF. Hopefully from a place of honesty and openness one can grow and improve while also connecting with others. We all deal with our own shit. We are all hypocrites and liars and dickheads and bitches and alcoholics and treat our spouses like garbage. We – as in YOU and I, along with everyone else – need improvement. I hardly ever talk about it because I'm a garbage Christian, but I do believe that this improvement can only really be attained through Jesus. I fight it all the time. I would venture to say I rarely improve as a person. Maybe I am in a decade long period of letting all my bullshit out and trying to come to terms with it. I pray that I mature one day. I pray that I am not a miserable fuck one day and that my kids can look to me as a source of strength and maybe even…a role model? Ugh. What a disgusting phrase.

No, I'm not saying that the only way to be a decent person is to be a Christian. We live in a society and you can indeed be a nice and "good" person without religion. Nice and good. Whatever the hell that means. I suppose therein lies the problem with me - I'm a cynic.

But let me sound off like an Instagram bio here for a second: I'm a lover of beautiful things. Of buildings and art and music. Of sunsets off the cove of La Jolla, CA. Great film and literature can move me to tears and does so on a regular basis. I'm a husband and I love my wife and it's beyond me how she is able to love me. I'm a father and I love my kids and sometimes I want to cry because I'm certain I am failing them in every possible way. I'm a dreamer. I dreamed of playing music and then I dreamed of being a writer. I dream of being rich. I dream of being respected and credentialed. I dream of success and a house with a designer kitchen and a Texas style BBQ pit and a wood fire oven in my backyard.

What in the HELL does this have to do with Emery. Well - everything.

Emery consists of my friends. As you will soon read, I have toured with them as both a peer and employee. I have also shared beers on their bus as a friend when they stop through town. I have worked on copious amounts of projects with Matt and Toby through BC. To top it all off, now Toby lives in my city and our wives like each other. I have a very personal connection to this group of people that the world knows as Emery. All those sappy things I wrote in the last paragraph influence my real life relationships, because Emery is a real life relationship for me. That's why I have to ability to write this book from a position of authority and vulnerability.

Matt has let some people read parts of the book to gauge reaction. This has been sobering for me and forced me to look at the way I communicate. Let me explain.

I like the book. I think I wrote the book I set out to write. I think YOU will like the book too, as long as your expectations are set correctly. I go into this in more of a harsh manner in the first chapter, but let me tell you what this book is not:

It is NOT a biography.

It is NOT a precise historical account with absolutely no bias or commentary whatsoever.

It is NOT happy go lucky and a praise book of your favorite band, Emery.

So what IS this book?

It IS honest.

It IS from the view of someone who really knows the ins and outs of the world that Emery comes from.

It IS supposed to be entertaining and tongue and cheek at times.

It IS a book that provides a ton of history and great quotes from band members.

It IS a book by ME and my voice and opinions permeate through every word you will read.

It IS a book about Emery. Just maybe not the one you thought it would be.

Most publishers would make me rewrite the entire book if I felt like I had to communicate all these things as a disclaimer. But BC Words is not most publishers. Thank God for that, because I like this book the way it is. It IS the book I set out to write.

I hate the feeling of needing people to like me. I'm here to tell you that it's okay if you don't like me when you read this. I get it. But hopefully this prologue has helped you understand who I am. I'm complex, happy, and unhappy Even when I'm writing a book about someone else, I can't help but talk about myself.

I want you to know that I genuinely appreciate you taking the time to read this. I REALLY appreciate that you spent your money on it, because this helps me provide for my family. So try this: anytime you think I'm being an ass towards your favorite band Emery, remember that I have a daughter named Magnolia and a son named Buddy. Actually, by the time you guys are reading this I will have another son…hopefully his name is Chipper Jones Lunsford. Now, think of that guy. Think of a guy that your favorite band considers a friend. Think of your friend that is kind of an ass but you really enjoy his company because he shakes things up a little bit. Also remember that I am just a keyboard warrior. In person I think I'm actually pretty friendly, if not incredibly socially awkward and non confrontational.

So without further ado, here is my book about Emery.

—

[1]

EMERY???

I'm not a fan of the band Emery. So why the hell would I write a book about a band I don't even like? Ok let's dig into that a little bit. Don't write me off. I have a perfectly legitimate explanation for why I've undertaken this project.

My name is Aaron Lunsford, and I played drums in a band called As Cities Burn. Some of you may have read my previous book about my own life experiences playing in a band. I've played shows, been friends, and embarked on very long tours with A LOT of bands - too many to count and too many to even want to remember. It's the reason I don't go to shows anymore. Because music has so oversaturated my life, I can't handle listening to much music these days. Unless it's Ryan Adams at The Ryman in Nashville of course.

Out of all the bands I've known and spent drunken nights with exchanging stories and forming special (yet, inevitably ephemeral) bonds, I would say I have been an actual fan of four bands. These are bands I genuinely liked in such a way that I might buy their t-shirt or record. Jonezetta, Brandtson, mewithoutYou, and Tallhart. That's pretty much it.

"But Aaron! You've toured with Underoath, The Bled, Mayday Parade, Pierce the Veil, Gym Class Heroes, Dredg, and THE MASTERS OF ROCK - EMERY."

Yes, I most definitely have. Here I go, stroking my own balls about my impressive music career, while at the same time talking shit about my friends that are making themselves extremely available for the purposes of this book.

But allow me to persuade you of something. *You don't want a fan to write this book.* Can you imagine what a terrible story that would be? A fan would have never been berated by the lead singer of Emery in front of his new girlfriend for failing to arrange parking for the bus on a night off in Santa Monica while serving as Tour Manager. A fan doesn't know what it is like to be a fly on the wall in a truck stop outside of Memphis while Emery very colorfully, southernly, and loudly discuss why in the hell they are going to have to pay a management commission of $40K on a tour that basically lost money. A fan hasn't spent years of his or her life living on a bus with Emery. A fan hasn't had the opportunity to be the sounding board for individual members of Emery to express their frustrations with regards to their band-mates. Fans have virtually no valuable perspective on the matters of a band other than whether or not they enjoyed said band's most recent record release or live show or t-shirt design. *You don't want a fan to write this book.*

So who the hell am I other than the asshole drummer who upon first look thinks all his friends' bands suck? I am the guy who has been incredibly fortunate enough to have spent a significant portion of my adult life getting to know Emery in the ways I've just mentioned. I have toured with Emery as a peer musician. I have tour managed Emery. I MANAGED Emery (I'll explain the difference at some point in this book). I have been the benefactor of being a member of a supporting band on one of Emery's biggest headlining tours of their career. More recently, I had the pleasure of watching Emery OPEN for my dumb-ass band for a few weeks. And believe it or not, Emery has been present for the two absolute worst days of my entire life. To be honest, I don't know if they are a blessing or a curse.

*****

In January of 2004 I was in Baton

Rouge, LA, waiting to embark on the next As Cities Burn tour. There was this total shit hole of a house we used to crash at near the LSU campus. The floors were literally caving in, and all the hardcore house shows didn't help. Since we were always on the road, it wasn't really possible to get jobs while we were home. Quitting after two weeks of employment is typically frowned upon, therefore giving us a great excuse to just sit around, jack off, and not drink alcohol like good Christian boys. Saving us from boredom and poverty was Cici's pizza, Jack in the Box, and the Internet.

My journey to living in this hellhole band crash pad was pretty typical for a Christian kid who was into music. I grew up listening to Tooth and Nail bands, mostly of the pop punk variety. Eventually I ventured into the brilliance of Further Seems Forever. My dream was to be in a band and get signed to Tooth and Nail Records. So in the interest of seeing where the music industry was heading, I kept a pretty good eye on the bands that Tooth and Nail was signing. Every time a new band would get signed, I would obsess over trying to figure out the path they took to landing a record deal; every day trying to understand what it was going to take to fulfill my dream.

So what does a boy do when he dislikes the bands his dream label is signing? I remember the first time I saw the video for "Walls" by Emery. I remember the scorn I felt. I thought to myself, "WHO? THEM?!!!". This is what Tooth and Nail wants? A bunch of old dudes dressed all preppy with a well produced record? THIS IS BULLSHIT. I hated Emery. I didn't like the song. I didn't like the video. I didn't like their "image".

Most of all, I was jealous. I thought we (As Cities Burn) were better than they were (we weren't). I thought we deserved a record deal before they did (we didn't).

"That should be us…", I thought. Here we are, back to me talking shit about your favorite band and alienating the very readers I am trying to sell books to. Are you still with me? *Are you listening?*

Remember when I said I was a fan of only four bands I've ever toured with? Well, it wasn't just Emery that I didn't like. This feeling of jealousy wasn't about Emery. Underoath. Beloved. Norma Jean. Anberlin. The Chariot. He Is Legend. Showbread. Haste the Day. Dead Poetic. All bands on the label As Cities Burn would eventually sign with that I wasn't a fan of.

You know what I figured out? It was okay to feel this way. Well not the jealousy, that was stupid. But not being a fan of all my future label mates didn't fucking matter. I loved Jimmy Eat World. I didn't have to love the music of my peers. My colleagues. My brethren. Jimmy Eat World was not my peer. We were never venturing into their circle. All these new Tooth and Nail bands? They would be my peers and they probably didn't like my band either, and that's ok. None of us were there to be fans of each other's bands. In fact, I have always thought FOR SURE that Toby Morrell, the singer for Emery, does not like As Cities Burn. That's okay, too.

These feelings evolve. Once you realize that it's not about being a fan of the bands you are touring with and developing relationships with, you find freedom. The freedom to find something vastly more important that fandom:

Respect.

I was able to learn to appreciate and respect all these bands from a professional point of view. I was able to learn to take great joy in observing what other bands did well that my band did not. Call it growing up or call it not being such a fucking elitist asshole. Either way, I'm glad I ended up learning respect. More than any of these label mates I mentioned, I respect the hell out of Emery.

I don't actually think that Emery sucks. If I thought that, I wouldn't be able to look them in the eye. It would feel awkward. No, no, far from sucking. *Emery is fucking amazing.*

Emery as a whole is an immensely talented group of individuals. They are smart. They are calculated. They are excellent businessmen. They are creative. They know what they want and they know how to get what they want. I do not have more respect for any other band I have ever had the opportunity to know. Emery is a well-oiled machine and a model for long term success in a shit business.

Emery's sound was not groundbreaking relative to their contemporaries. In this way, they've never been a "band's band." That means that they weren't doing some earthshattering, original shit that every band in the scene adored, regardless of their ultimate fan popularity.

Respect.

That's what really matters between peers. The respect that Emery garners has much more to do with them as people. They are a phenomenally interesting group of guys to be around. Their personalities transcend genres and boundaries of "cool". The truth is, once you get on a bus and crack open a beer, nobody gives a shit about the songs you wrote if you are a good dude to hang around. Conversation on the bus or backstage trumps the music. Always and forever. Why? Because for 23 hours a day on tour, it's just hanging. Sleeping. Eating. Drinking copious amounts of beer. Who gives a shit about the music? It's not like we were all on tour with Jimmy Eat World.

In this regard: the hangs, the conversation, the

drinking - Emery are the motherfucking Beatles. They are Nirvana. They have changed the way band dudes hang on tour for all of eternity. The most influential conversationalists of their time. The lounge on the Emery bus is basically "Pet Sounds" but for talking with absurd southern accents and an ice chest with endless amounts of Bud Light thanks to trusty tour managers. You think Freddie Mercury is a legend? Spend ten minutes discussing the nuances of band economics with Matt Carter and Toby Morrell and you'll find a new definition of entertainment. Many years ago I suggested they start a podcast, and I probably wasn't the only one.

*****

Emery is an unlikely success story, in my professional opinion. I could make one point and win this argument immediately: all of the founding members of Emery graduated from college before the band even really got going. In my experience, pursuing life as a touring musician is a result of deciding to drop out of college and throw caution into the wind. There is no back up plan. Getting a record deal and finding success as a nationally known artist is the only option. Usually, after completing a quality education, most grown men just fall into the status quo of "real jobs," marriage, and having kids. So how in the hell did Emery avoid the "status quo"? Determination? Or destiny?

Typically, a group of qualified individuals such as Emery have no place in this world of losers and fuck ups. However, as a result of pragmatism, wisdom, and a desire for an adventure, Emery saw starting a band as a viable career option. They *made* it be so.

Matt could have been a doctor, or taken over his father's business. Toby could have married a college sweetheart and became a music teacher at a confederate flag-flying South Carolina high school. Devin could have displayed his talents on American Idol and become an R&B superstar the likes of which we haven't seen since R. Kelly got trapped in the closet. Chopper could have moved to Nashville and found work as a hired gun. Seth could have…well I don't know Seth really at all, because I haven't interviewed him yet and he quit the band before As Cities Burn ever toured with Emery. But I'm sure he could have done something! Josh is a beautiful man, and modeling would not have been out of reach for him. Actually, he should probably go ahead and check that out even now. Old Spice needs old men to model cologne, I think.

These guys could have done anything, but they decided to start a screamo band and move to Seattle. Why? Because they're dumbass rednecks from South Carolina who didn't know any better. It worked, though. In the end, Emery would sell hundreds of thousands of records for Tooth and Nail.

The best super hero movies are the origins stories. We love to know where legends come from. At least I do. Sometimes going back to the beginning is the only way to get the full picture of something we love. So how *did* Emery become "The Masters of Rock"?

2

SONS OF THE CONFEDERACY

I'm sitting in Matt Carter's living room in
Seattle, Washington sipping on a Sierra Nevada "Torpedo
IPA". Seattle is only a continental coast away, but it feels
like a million miles from where Emery started. Seattle,
the ultra progressive hotbed with their tolerance, coffee,
and $15/hour minimum-wage. Seattle couldn't be more
opposite of Greer, South Carolina. But no matter where a
band comes from, everyone has a story about the music
that changed their outlook and trajectory forever. Hearing
a band that caused them to pick up drumsticks or a guitar

for the first time. For some, it's raiding your cool uncle's record collection. Or, a friend loans you a CD of a band you've never heard. For others, it's a 2 AM rabbit-hole journey of discovering new bands online. Or sometimes-- if you're old like the members of Emery--it's hearing a new band on the radio.

"There wasn't [sic] other bands at our school," Matt says of the "music scene" in Greer. "I'm really certain that we were the first band ever at our high school...at all," Matt says with a shrug. *But what about the indie and punk scene in the area?*, I ask. Surely the guitarist for a band that was a giant in the screamo/indie hardcore, or whatever, scene grew up playing in punk bands and listening to Green Day. There must have been some sort of "scene," right? "I had heard of the word 'punk'," Matt said. "I just assumed that meant green mohawk and leather spikes." But Matt's ignorance of the punk scene was quite perplexing to me. I had expected him to tell stories similar to my own adolescence. Like remembering going to shows as a teenager, or buying that first Green Day CD. How could Matt Carter of Emery, a band who has played hundreds if not thousands of shows, have not grown up *going* to shows? He replied, "I would have never known the word 'shows'...I knew that Metallica played *concerts.*"

So there were no "shows", and no discernable punk scene to speak of, at least from Matt's perspective. However, he was in a band throughout high school called "Simply Waynes", founded by Matt, Seth and Dev. In a town like Greer, South Carolina, no one plays "shows" within a local "scene". Instead, you get and play "gigs". Maybe the difference between a show and a gig is the difference between active listening (show), and people who are present but uninterested in music, while live music is being played (gig). As Seth recounted it, his sweet grandma showed her love for him by allowing Simply Waynes to play a Christmas party "gig". "My grandma was kind of cool and she would let us play Christmas parties at her house," he said. "So we were playing Nirvana songs for family and neighbors."

Aha! Of course they'd heard Nirvana! They were on the fucking radio. Everybody knew Nirvana. It required no ambition of their own to discover the band that changed rock history in the nineties. I can relate a little bit, though. My nowhere town in Arkansas wasn't that different than Greer, really. I just had an older friend who figured out that Christian book stores carried punk rock and ska records. Otherwise, the radio would have been all I knew.

"Just being in a small town, it's just nuthin'," Matt said in his most southern drawl. "But you didn't know it was nuthin'." He couldn't be more spot on. You can't miss what you don't know.

*****

Interstate 85 runs just to the south of Greer, which is situated in between Greenville and Spartanburg. For reference, Greenville is towards Atlanta, and Spartanburg is in the direction of Charlotte. Northwest South Carolina is sometimes referred to as the Appalachian or Blue Ridge region. Most of South Carolina is what the inhabitants refer to as "low country," meaning it's pretty much at sea level. Greer, however, is nestled right up to the foothills of the Appalachians with Asheville, North Carolina, which is just a short drive north into the mountains. I hadn't realized how mountainous the area was until I visited Matt's parents a few years ago. Matt and Devin are from Blue Ridge, and it feels like the absolute middle of nowhere. They were "neighbors," having grown up just 1.2 miles apart. In Blue Ridge, 1.2 miles is basically next door.

As of 2015, the population of Greer is slightly under 30,000 people. In 2000, a few years after all the founding members of Emery had graduated high school, the population was only 16,000. I'm going to take a wild guess that in the year 2000, Starbucks hadn't set up shop yet.

Greer is the kind of town where people are "born and raised", and "born and raised" basically just means poverty and a local business economy. T-ball teams in places like Greer are sponsored by Bob's Electric or A&E Credit Union.

Often a city or town's economy is built around a single industry. For instance, the textile industry was huge in Greer after WWII up until the 1970's. Then, foreign manufacturing competition led to economic decline. But Greer's economy would bounce back and attract new industries. Today, they have the only BMW factory in North America, as well as the South Carolina Inland Port, which ships out containers to Charleston via railroad.

All this to say that Greer is still your typical Southern rural town with lots of small businesses, churches, and white people. People who were *born and raised.* Because when you are poor, you can't go anywhere. When your dad is Bob and he owns Bob's Electric, you are staying put. These are roughly the kind of factors that allowed Matt, Devin and Seth to literally grow up together since t-ball. Like, they actually played t-ball together.

Toby and Chopper were older than these three, but they were also basically lifelong friends. Everybody's families knew each other. This was some real small town shit. confused?

Maybe it's time to define the characters of this literature you are consuming. Before we get too far in, let me lay out a few necessary facts and details that will make this book a lot easier to follow.

We have established that Matt, Devin, Seth, Chopper (Joel), and Toby are all from Greer, SC, but *who* are these people. Let's take it one by one. The rundown of Emery is:

Matt Carter (Greer, SC) - guitarist and instrumentation as well as one of three primary songwriters.

Devin Shelton (Greer, SC) - guitarist/vocals and a primary songwriter

Seth Studley (Greer, SC) - original drummer

Joel Greene (Chopper) (Greer, SC) - bass guitar and background vocals

Toby Morrell (Greer, SC) - lead vocals and songwriter.

Josh Head (Seattle, WA) - keyboards, dancer, good looking guy

Dave Powell (Indianapolis, IN) – current drummer

God willing, you just experienced the most boring segment of the book. If you are reading this now, it means I didn't figure out a better way to lay out that most basic information. Now we can move forward with the understanding that when I refer to one of these names, there is no question who I may be talking about.

For the purpose of discussing Greer, SC, we have already broken Emery up into two groups: Matt, Devin and Seth vs. Toby and Chopper. Not like a battle of the rednecks. The "vs." is for dramatic literary effect.

Seth came as close to growing up with Toby as one could without actually knowing him. "I used to ride bikes back behind his house on trails," he said. "We didn't know each other because we went to different schools, but I used to hang out 100 yards behind his house." Even more bizarre was the connection to Toby and Joel that Seth unknowingly had through his mom. "My mom was a teacher at Joel and Toby's school. My mom knew Joel and Toby before I did." Seth's future bandmates were more likely to have been sent to the principal's office by his mom than to ever jam some shitty 90's grunge songs in a garage with him.

Matt and Toby, who have grown to be closer friends than any other original members of the band over the years due to a continued professional partnership (and even a musical project called "Matt & Toby") didn't know each other during their youth either. "I knew of him," Matt said, when I asked about their relationship prior to college. Toby sang in the school chorus and for whatever reason Matt was familiar with him because of that. I imagine this familiarity being similar to the mild familiarity one may have with an upperclassman that they have never spoken to but have seen their picture in the yearbook.

I started playing in bands when I was 14 years old in a band called "Arkanska". Most of us who devoted our lives to "making it" in a band started in basements and garages around the same age. But as I said, Emery's success story is an atypical one.

Seth got to play his grandma's Christmas parties. But Devin, for instance, wasn't even a musician in high school. He was just a singer in the high school chorus. "I didn't play music at all until college," he said. Devin was "never even interested, really" in being in a band.

Even though Devin and Matt "grew up together" as I keep mentioning, Devin specified that he didn't actually become friends with Matt until late into high school. On the other hand, he knew Seth quite well all the way up through high school. Since Seth and Matt were friends, and Seth and Devin were friends, Devin was able to get to know Matt through Seth.

It's remarkable that any of these guys ever learned about other types of music outside of Nirvana and Silverchair. When I ask the members about their introduction to hardcore or emo, all I get is, "We didn't know that type of music existed." Since all the Emery members had graduated high school by 1997, their formative years weren't spent downloading songs on Napster and getting acquainted with the internet like my friends and I did. The idea of being in a band for a living didn't register to the members of Emery, because only rock stars from Seattle are professional musicians. These Sons of the Confederacy were completely clueless to the fact that while they were listening to radio rock in the mid-Nineties, that a kid named Brandon Ebel was on the verge of building a record label in Seattle that would change their lives forever.

*****

***To understand Emery**,* we must understand where they came from. There is no other place to start. Even though in 2016 there are technically only two members still in the band that were raised in Greer, the influence of the region is prevalent in the makeup of the dynamics of Emery. South Carolina is the fabric from which the original members of Emery were sewn. This can never be undone.

At the heart of everything, I know for a fact I would not enjoy the company of Emery like I do were it not for their accents and southern upbringing. It's very difficult to put in the words, but I'll try. (Oh the irony of writing a book and having to write that.). It's a feeling of familiarity and understanding. In some ways, southerners know each other before they know each other. There is a level of comfortability, especially when we found ourselves outside of Dixie. There is nothing better than being in California and running into somebody from Jackson or Memphis or Greer, SC. The conversation immediately has the opportunity to switch towards BBQ and allowing your southern accent to shine.

I could probably do a whole chapter on southern accents. I won't bore you, but it is worth noting how defining the accents of Emery have been throughout their career. Most amazingly, even though they have toured the world, lived in Seattle, married girls from the midwest and so on…Matt, Devin, Seth, Toby and Chopper have not lost a shred of their accents from what I can tell. They are thick and embedded deep in their vocal chords. In contrast, my accent comes and goes depending on who I'm talking to. It's not for a lack of being genuine, it's just a quirk. My mom always tried to get me to not sound southern. I know the reasons, but this isn't a memoir about my upbringing so I will save that for another book. But yes, I have a fluctuating southern accent. I love it. I wish it was always there. Sometimes I'll get off the phone with Matt and then walk into the next room and start talking to my wife and she will say to me, "Have you been talking to Emery?". These guys bring out my accent better than anyone and I love them for it.

So now I come to the point of posing the question to which an answer has escaped me through all my research and conversations with the members of Emery.

How in the hell do five guys from a nothing town all stick together to start an internationally known screamo band?

"Yeah I guess it is weird," Seth says with genuine curiosity, "I wonder what other bands are from the Greer

area that are as big, or close to as big, as Emery....
probably nobody?" Seth seems to have never even
thought about it before. A lightbulb goes off in Seth's
head. "Hootie and The Blowfish?" They are from
Columbia, SC. Not Greer.

Matt laughed his ass off upon hearing Seth's Hootie
ponderings and excitedly mocked Seth's answer. "You
could name one band from our STATE that got a record
deal, and THAT WAS IN 1990!" He continued, "On
some level you say, 'Ooh how could there be that much
talent that close together,' but rock bands aren't really
that talented." That's actually pretty spot on folks.
What's that saying that jazz musicians throw around?
'He didn't have any talent so he joined a rock band'?

I suppose there is a genuinely humble attitude
underneath this lack of understanding of the
improbability of a band like Emery ever even existing.
But I really believe this is the cornerstone of their story;
where they are from, their lack of access to music and
shows. If Emery were from Los Angeles, they wouldn't
have a compelling story. You need an interesting reason
to cover an LA band, like the drummer murdered his
neighbor or the singer is a drug kingpin . Tons of bands

are from the West Coast. It's a thing.

Greer, South Carolina is not a "thing" in any way, shape, or form. For that reason, I declare the existence and career of Emery either an act of God, a result of an incredible work ethic, or just dumb luck. I am going to guess that it is a combination of all three. But if you are thinking these guys all graduated high school and fell right into the band life, you would be mistaken. These fuckers went on to learn some stuff. These fuckers went to college. In the band world, this truly IS an act of God.

3

ZOD, the Benevolent

The first time I met Matt, he was less
than impressed with me as a human, as far as I could tell.
I chronicle this story in my previous book, but once I
tried to butter Matt up with small talk in hopes that he'd
help my band, As Cities Burn, get an opening slot at a
Tooth and Nail festival show with Emery, Anberlin,
mewithoutYou, and Watashi Wa. Matt was in the parking
lot of the venue sorting merch, and I walked up, hands in
my pockets, and said, "So…this is the Tooth and Nail
Tour huh?".

He didn't even look up from his task and simply
replied, "Yep." I was 21 years old with nothing to offer

anyone. I was a taker. I was hoping to get something out of talking to one of the guys in a band. *Please pretty please help get my band on this show, out of the goodness of your heart!*

There we were in the parking lot of an all ages venue. I had nothing to talk about and Matt went on with sorting merch.

Matt Carter knows what he knows. He doesn't know what he doesn't know, which isn't much because well, Matt Carter thinks he knows EVERYTHING. I'll give it to him though, I genuinely think he might be in the top five smartest people I know category. He is full of knowledge regarding things you have never heard him talk about before. Whether his knowledge is valuable or not is up to those who choose to listen. Some think he lacks credibility because he has an accent so redneck and so foreign to his Seattle neighbors they think he is from England. But I would say, I think Matt's qualities are wasted in the music industry. In my opinion, the music industry is mostly a bunch of clowns doing nothing of consequence with a few smart people scattered throughout. Matt should have continued on to become a doctor, as he originally planned. The world would be a better place for it. Instead, he helped start a screamo band. Way to pull your weight, buddy.

I don't get the sense that Matt needs to feel like he must benefit from every interaction, but he will certainly try. This is because he's a master manipulator. I'll qualify that by saying he is a *benevolent* master manipulator. In fact, I think I was manipulated into writing this book. My memory is blurry, but months before starting this book project, I was talking to Matt about writing a book focused on a particular era of Tooth and Nail bands. During the course of this conversation, Matt convinced me to write a book exclusively about Emery. But not directly. The idea was planted deep inside, like inception. Perhaps in a conversation on the tour bus years ago or during one of our frequent phone calls discussing other matters.

Before I even realized what happened, I was pitching Matt an idea for a book that was his idea to begin with. Amazing. But I greatly benefited from the manipulation because I get to be published.

I've enjoyed watching Matt's skills of manipulation evolve over the years. But again, when I use the word "manipulation" I don't mean to take a jab at Matt. I actually mean it as a compliment. Maybe "shrewd" is a better word. In the same way that Matt got me to write this book without me understanding how he was influencing me, he has surrounded himself with many talented people in which both parties mutually benefit from one another.

Toby is by far Matt's longest and most successful manipulation experiment. How else do you get a man who just turned 40 years old to keep making Emery records, start a podcast and a media company that puts out books, records, podcasts, and God knows what else? Toby doesn't want to do any of those things, but Matt is able to make Toby see that he needs to. I don't foresee a scenario when Matt doesn't have a hand in something Toby is doing, directly or indirectly.

*****

"That phone is 128 gigabytes? That's a lot." I had just recently acquired the iPhone 6S Plus. It's massive. And I have an Otterbox on it so the sleekness of the design is totally lost. I boast about the amount of storage on the phone, to which Matt is mildly impressed.

"Yeah man this way I never have to worry about having space to take pictures of the kids. Drives me crazy when I have to delete a video before snapping a pic." Matt might have been interested in discussing this further if I happened to be the one that figured out how to put 128GB of storage on a phone. But I'm just sitting in his living room to interview him about his band. Back to business we go.

At the time of our interview, Matt had recently purchased a home on the north side of Seattle for an astronomical amount of money for the square footage. It's the price you pay to live in one of the most beautiful and comfortable cities in the country. Matt's wife, Bridget, was kind enough to run to the store and grab a six pack of IPA for Matt and I to share. She's from Seattle which obviously plays a part in Matt's choice choosing to pay steeply to stay there. Matt has addressed the issue practically in that at least his rent can't go up now and they get to stay in the city limits and stay close to all the things that make Seattle a cool place to live. He is big on his daughter growing up in a diverse setting. For all its downfalls, city living will certainly not produce a child that can be labeled as "sheltered". Matt's feelings on the matter are actually quite influential in keeping me living in East Nashville where I hear gun shots nightly and the police helicopter - AKA "Ghetto Bird" as it is so affectionately known as on the neighborhood Facebook page - circling my house several times a week. But dammit we have Mexican immigrants making tacos and black people making BBQ and real Nashville Hot Chicken. The white suburbs south of town have Chipotle and Chick-Fil-A. I am fucking addicted to that queer hating chicken sandwich.

Seattle is twenty times more interesting a place to live in terms of "diversity". It's worth it to pay $450 a square foot just for the access to a decent bowl of asian noodles or sushi that didn't come from a fish farm. I also really love that Matt is the whitest man on earth. Pale as a ghost. We've addressed the accent. His fashion and taste are right in line with a typical white dude from a successful screamo band. Matt's wife is some amount of Latino and some amount of African American, leaving the couple with a beautiful little brown skinned daughter. Matt is so freaking white that it was necessary that he mate with a person of color so that his offspring would be visible without use of infrared goggles to detect the presence of a little white ghost baby.

It says a lot about Matt and his lack of fear for the unknown that he came from such a small backwoods place and feels comfortable navigating a large West Coast city in an interracial relationship. Most people from a town like Greer, South Carolina don't leave, and they certainly aren't bringing home a significant other of a different skin color.

People often mistake Matt's accent to mean he's a dumb redneck, which he is not. He comes from educated folks. His father is a civil engineer and his mother studied social work. See, there are even folks from Greer, South Carolina who went to college, and the Carter family likely falls into the category of "elite" when it comes to education and prosperity. Yes, they have money.

Matt likes his life in Seattle. But because of his lack of fear, he could also totally like doing something else; like live in a tiny house or RV. Live uprooted and communally. I've even heard him ponder moving to Indianapolis, Indiana because he figures he would be like a big fish in a small pond. He'd be able to dominate all those little Midwestern weirdos. But if you hang out in Matt's house for long, you learn he doesn't have a lot of

control over things. He always refers to his Seattle
residence as his "wife's house." It's like he is just along
for the ride, but willingly. I don't mean to suggest some
sort of dysfunction in his marriage. It's not that at all. I'm
saying he knows how to roll with it. Bridget and his
three-year-old daughter, Georgia, are running the show.
It's the girls' world and Matt is just living in it. At the
writing of this book, Matt and Bridget are expecting their
second child. God Bless him, now he's really
outnumbered.

"Around here we want to make a house and get it
better, and probably get a better car. It's a thing. It's a
normal thing." From Matt's vantage point, comparing the
communal lifestyle of the band to his life now boils down
to "a thing" to do. "What are we trying to do? I mean, we
will get better glasses, eat nicer food from Whole Foods.
We're doing a certain thing here. I don't actually think
it's better. It's just what this three person family is on the
train of." The son of a bitch is even pragmatic about the
direction of his family. Family is just something to do.
You have to do *something*, so what's the difference if that
something is shopping at Whole Foods and playing
house? With that said, whatever Matt finds himself doing,

he will fully get on board to make it fun and successful; whether it's building out his garage into a podcasting and recording studio, or installing heated floors in his kitchen (they are amazing to walk on in the morning). Matt is an all aboard type of guy when it comes to hopping on the various trains of life. Emery is a train. Marriage is a train. BadChristian is a train.

I would say that Matt is a great motivator to get groups of people excited about any particular project. There is no better example of this than the legendary ZP Casino - which operated on Emery's converted MCI charter bus

The ZP Casino story could be a book all its own. "ZP" stands for "Zod/Powell". Zod is Matt's nickname. The story goes that Emery's bassist, Joel, decided to give himself the nickname "Chopper" for no specific reason other than he thought it was a nice fit, to which Matt suggested that if people could just give themselves nicknames, then he might as well go by Zod - the namesake of which derives from the Superman villain from Krypton, Zod. Powell is Dave the drummer's last name, and these two were official partners in the business of the ZP Casino.

Gambling is just something you do when you're on tour – dice, cards, and poker. On any given day, in any given green room across the country, you are bound to find some smelly dudes kneeled on a beer, piss, and cum stained floor rolling dice for dollar bills. Matt and Dave decided to take this one step further after a trip to Vegas in which I introduced them to the best gambling game of all, craps.

Craps is the ultimate party game. Unless you are the asshole betting on the "Don't Come" line, everybody wins together and everybody loses together. It's hi fives and hugs, or sighing and despair. Seriously, don't be the asshole betting against the group. Although Matt likes to gamble a little bit, he really enjoys watching other people gamble, no matter if they win or lose. Starting ZP Casino was a totally selfish endeavor in this way, because not only would he make money because the house always wins, he would take great joy in watching his friends and tour mates make or lose money.

Originally, the ZP Casino was pretty basic. Matt made Dave a partner because Dave was willing, and Dave is likewise a guy who will hop on the train of fun if somebody is pushing it. Craps was a hit in Vegas, and lots of people can play at once. So they built a table out of the cardboard from old merch boxes, and used a sharpie to draw on all the different bets you could make. The bus had a pull down shade that they used to write down the odds for each bet for all to see.

Matt and Dave are smart businessmen. They decided to build the casino up slow. All the money they made from the casino was put back into the casino. They bought dealer visors. They upgraded the table by putting a black sheet over plywood and getting some red fabric to create the betting space. The walls of the table that you would roll the dice against were still made from cardboard but they were colored completely black. It was a thing of beauty. Beers were free, just like at a casino. God Bless tour catering budgets.

When I was tour managing Emery, it was my job to alert the rest of the bands on the tour about what time the casino would be opening. Most of the time, the casino was open on days off or after shows late at night. If folks were eager to lose money, Matt and Dave would open the casino before the show. Matt would convince the opening bands to follow us to wherever we were spending the day off to create a bigger pool of customers. The bets were small. Small enough so you could play for a long time without going broke. The minimum bet was only a nickel. I, for one, pretty much always bet way more than that. You could see Matt get nervous when you wanted to throw down ten dollars on the "Come" line - which is the place on the craps table one would make a basic bet. Not because ten dollars is a lot of money, but in proportion to the amount that most people would bet, winning even money on a ten-dollar bet could wipe out twenty five percent of the house winnings. It was fun to see Matt lose.

Man, I loved watching Matt lose money on his casino. He did it with such grace and integrity. He assumed the risk. The entertainment value was enough. You didn't have to worry about the house paying up, even if that meant Matt and Dave had to dip into their per diems to cover their losses. The great thing was that if the players won big one night, you could be damn sure Matt and Dave would be back the next night to try and recoup. Anytime ZP Casino was open for business was a good time. I would have to say it's Matt's greatest contribution to life on the road.

*****

I never negotiate with Matt on the phone.

His game verbal communication game is strong. If you
want to "win" against Matt, you've got to get him on
email or text. He talks too fast. He pauses too long after
you speak and it makes you second-guess yourself.
Sometimes he talks so much you can't even get a word in
and end up agreeing with him because you have nothing
to interject, or you don't know how to proceed in making
your case. When asking for an advance for this book
from BC Words - the publishing division of BadChristian
- I didn't even bother calling. Whatever I was asking for,
Matt would have successfully convinced me of another
plan.

This is where the master manipulator side of Matt
comes into play. He has a knack for getting to people
when they are down on their luck. He offers something
helpful, but he benefits from the arrangement. I first went
on tour to work for Emery only a couple months after my
first marriage crashed and burned. I was in the dumps and
Matt knew it. We knew each other fairly well at that point
since we'd done multiple tours together. He called me on

a cold night in November, 2009 just about a week before Emery left on a tour opening for Underoath and August Burns Red. I had just moved to Nashville from Baton Rouge seeking to move on from my failed marriage. I had only been there a few days when I got the call. Matt asked what I thought I could do for them on tour.

"Well…I think I could definitely tour manage or do merch or something," I said. They already had Peter "Pizza" Sellers doing merch and TM.

"Well, obviously I can load in and set up drums and stuff like that." But paying a drum tech wasn't really in the budget at that point in Emery's career (this was when their third record, "I'm Only a Man" kind of tanked sales-wise and they didn't have a lot of extra cash).

"Could you tune guitars or set any of that stuff up?" Matt asked.

"Well I'm sure you could teach me…" I said. He had me. He wanted the extra hand on tour, and he knew I was down on my luck and looking for anything to do. I was virtually useless to them, but I could at least prevent

---

[1] *"Buyout" is money you get from the promoter of a show in place of catering so that you can go buy Jimmy Johns or pad thai.*

them from having to load in or load out their own gear. He would offer me $150 a week plus per diems and buyouts.[1] I didn't have shit else to do, and being on tour with Emery is damn fun. I said yes, of course. Matt won.

Matt knew he was doing right by me. I had no real value to offer Emery for what they were willing to pay. I had zero confidence in my life due to the whole failed marriage thing. I needed to go hang out with some friends on the road. This was a mutually beneficial situation. By the end of the tour, I had taken over tour manager duties and I got a bonus at the end.

Those who know Matt have also heard his other nickname, "The Benevolent Dictator". He is often accused in person, on the podcast, and online as someone who is a manipulative robot, lacking empathy or emotion like a Mr. Spock. It really is all an exaggeration. Of course Matt feels for people. It's just not in the same way that most people do. I've actually even noticed him actively trying to improve on many of the perceived negative qualities that he has been typecast into. I think some of this growth comes with fatherhood and the feeling of sharing something amazing with the rest of us normal humans. There is this understanding between fathers that humanizes us all and helps us realize the struggles that we all go through. When I came to Matt asking for an advance to write this book, Matt knew why I was really asking. It wasn't so I could buy video games, go to bars, or take a trip to the beach with some bros. I just wanted to feed my fucking kids. As a father himself, he got that. He could have negotiated down the asking price significantly. I would have said yes to just about any amount of money because I need to support my family.

But in this instance - and this is the big change I have noticed in Matt over the past couple years - he was willing to negotiate based on my actual value to him and not just the direness of my situation. Yeah I know that before I said I didn't have much to offer Emery as far as tour personnel value, but Matt was in a position to win that one no matter what. This time around, I do have responsibilities and life obligations I need to take care of. I had proven with my first book I wrote for BC that I could be valuable and financially viable as an author. Matt could have leveraged my life situation against me and I would have agreed to still do the book. Shit, maybe I would've agreed to do it for no advance at all. In that case it's simply an investment on my part. I make out a lot better in the end if I decide to write this book for no money up front. But, Matt heard my argument and agreed that I made a valid argument for getting paid some money in advance. He did try to talk me out of it. He did try to play a little bit of that benevolent dictator role, but in the end he knew I was right to ask for the advance. I think he respected the confidence shown by asking. Through email. Good God, not on the phone. Maybe email lacks balls. Go ahead and judge me.

*****

I worry that this chapter is just one big dick suck of Matt's ghost white redneck cock, but for every bad thing I can say about Matt I am able to find redeeming qualities. The main one being that he is incredibly effective at convincing you why he isn't bad. His goal is to get you to think differently about something. He challenges and pushes you to be better. I don't agree with Matt on plenty of things. I could go back through hundreds of conversations or cite instances from the podcast that make me roll my eyes and call bullshit.

Like, I could never ever in a million years be in a band with Matt. He would want to tell me every fucking beat to play. Every fucking note. Every accent. He is God in the studio. He is God in BC world. He's running the show, and that's great. There is nobody better suited for it. Nobody in Emery or the BC world is going to make that shit go the way Matt will. I had to learn that working FOR Matt is not as fun as working WITH Matt.

I loved tour managing Emery. I fucking hated managing Emery. If you don't know the difference, there is a book called "All You Need to Know About the Music Business" that goes into great detail on these things. Basically the tour manager oversees all touring operations, while a manager oversees every single aspect of a band's business.. Actually when I say I loved tour managing Emery, I mean it was an incredible amount of fun. However, it still was not easy working for them. Now this may be a me thing. I have a sense that I am capable of things. Artistic and creative things. I may be delusional, but I have a sense that I am smarter than most people. I also have a sense that I am the worst employee known to man. It has become hard for me to work FOR people. However, I have found my wheelhouse in working with people, in being the TALENT per se. I think Matt has realized this and he stopped asking me to work for him.

He stopped asking me to do anything administrative. Anything day to day. As a result of this change, I am writing books, producing podcasts and documentaries, and happy with my professional relationship with Matt. I have arrived at a comfort level with the God of this little creative world that we work in where I can be myself. Where I can feel like I am contributing in a way that is valuable outside of simply keeping track of how much money Emery has made on a tour. No more walking little Mexican girls in South Texas to ATM's to prove to me that she has no money to pay Emery the rest of their guarantee. No more making sure the ice chest is filled to the brim with ice and beer. No more explaining to Matt why Emery is going on after their scheduled set time.

My conversation with Matt in Seattle at his home was like any number of conversations I've had with him. I just happened to be recording it. Earlier in the night, we went to get Indian food with his wife in a hip neighborhood of Seattle. The food was great and the conversation was fantastic. This conversation might have been even better than what I was able to record. It was free and natural. I wasn't interviewing him. We were just talking, like always. He told me many things that I could write. Some things would be unethical to repeat, while others I just don't remember. But I could go and sit down with Matt for beers and BBQ right now and get a conversation on tape just as interesting and revealing as the one we had at the Indian restaurants back in December of 2015. How many times do I have to say it? The dude is down to talk.

At the time of our interview, the last thing I asked Matt was, "Who's your favorite crew member?" I know almost all of Emery's crew personally and most all of them are fantastic people. "Crew members are these built in people that work for you that you get to give a hard time to and it's in to the culture and it's just great; if they can hang or handle it." After riffing on the benefits of good crew members for a few minutes, I can tell he's thinking about something. I don't know if it was a calculated decision. I don't know if it's true. I don't know if there was an angle to it. But he dove into it. Me, sitting in his living room drinking the beer he paid for, traveling and doing research on the money he fronted me, entertaining me for hours with his musings on the band and all the absurdity that comes with it...he goes for it.

"I mean there's a very, very, very real....very, very real sense...or argument...that...you're my favorite..." Matt quipped.

Master manipulator? What do you mean?

4

COLLEGE BOYS

If you listen to any member of Emery speak, you would think they were dumbass rednecks. Don't let the accents fool you. The boys from Emery are a pretty smart squad.

In fact Matt, Devin, Toby, Seth and Chopper ALL graduated college BEFORE starting Emery full time. In my experience, that just doesn't happen. The touring world is riddled with kids that didn't even graduate high school much less college. Others just went to college looking for 3 or 4 other dudes that wanted to drop that shit and go on tour. Finishing a degree is often not a part of the plan. This makes Emery, like, the smartest, most responsible screamo band of all time.

Winthrop University is a small, public liberal arts college in Rock Hill, South Carolina, and the dudes from Emery are probably their most notable alumni of all time (except for Andie MacDowell, the love interest of Bill Murray in the movie "Groundhog Day".) Toby and Chopper had already been attending Winthrop University for a couple years before Devin enrolled following his high school graduation in 1997.

Matt actually started at Clemson University, which leads me to say that I'm surprised he ever left. Matt and Toby are die hard Clemson fans, so the idea of actually having the opportunity to attend the school that you grew up idolizing seems too good to give up. But Matt did not last long at his family's alma mater. Instead, he dropped out of Clemson biology program—the stepping stone to pursuing a medical degree – and began attending Winthrop's music program.

"After the first year (of college) Matt left Clemson to come and do music." That's Devin talking about Matt ending up at Winthrop with him, Toby and Chopper. I asked Matt specifically why he left Clemson, the college that his father and sister also attended, so in other words -

a family tradition. "Ooh this is a good story," said Matt.

According to Matt, there were about 300 kids in his freshman class, and by the end of the year that number was down to about 120. That's an impressive attrition rate for first year of an undergraduate program. Matt was doing really well, hovering in the top 20% of his class. So what threw him off the course? Well there are two theories. One involves a music theory class. The other…girls.

"I took a music theory class as an elective my freshman year and I thought 'Oh yeah this is it', I just got it immediately," Matt said. "I could have taken the final exam on the first day of class and gotten a good grade." Matt had only been playing guitar for a couple years at this point, but for some reason, music theory clicked with him.

At the same time Matt was discovering he was basically a 19 year old redneck Mozart, Devin was chasing a girl named Lindsey. Lindsey had a best friend, Carrie, and Matt had taken a liking to her. The funniest part about this story is that both these girls had boyfriends. That didn't seem to matter to Devin or Matt. Depending on who you ask, it seems that Matt left the prospect of medical school and his beloved Clemson for a girl that had a boyfriend. After his first year at Clemson, he transferred to Winthrop.

"I'm inclined to say I left to go study music, because Clemson didn't have a music program like Winthrop," Matt insisted. "But if you ask somebody else, they might say it was for a girl." She never broke up with her boyfriend. It doesn't suit Matt to go chasing a girl. I would guess he genuinely left Clemson because his interests shifted. However, guys do crazy shit for the opportunity to see some boobs, so who knows.

Other than Seth, who actually went to the University of South Carolina at Spartanburg, you had every eventual member of Emery enrolled in the music program at Winthrop. Which brings me back to the sharpness of this group. I don't know if you have ever had friends that studied music in college, but it's a bitch. It's no cakewalk of a college degree. Like I said, don't let the accents fool you.

Devin and Toby had already become friends because they were both vocal performance majors. Once Matt transferred over to Winthrop, he started to become friends with Toby. Well…not immediately. Toby has discussed at length how he couldn't stand Matt when he first met him. "Who the fuck is this guy?" is more or less Toby's reaction to his first encounter with Matt. He believed Matt to be obnoxious and wanted little to do with him. "Yeah, but that's what he thinks about everybody," Matt told me when I asked about Toby not liking him at first. "That's 95 percent of the people he meets!"

I realized at that moment that there is nothing significant whatsoever about Toby's initial feelings towards Matt. Toby always starts at "people are bad." "His mom was not a trustworthy person, so he doesn't trust people," Matt said. "That way it's just safer." Eventually - if you are worthy - Toby warms up to you. Obviously, this was the case with Matt.

But one of the most important influences on the historical trajectory is Joey Svendsen. In reality, Joey was an original member of Emery; more original than Chopper or Seth. You could make an argument that he was the *founding* member of Emery. Joey was also a student at Winthrop, and he and Toby hit it off. Within weeks of meeting, friends and classmates were already referring to the duo as best friends. In 2016 terminology,

Toby and Joey had a bromance, and this is where the foundation of Emery's future sound really began to form.

*****

Whether you've met Joey in person, or have listened to him on the BadChristian Podcast, you may not take him for being an influencer of musical taste. But Joey is an absolute music influencer. He is always trying to bring everyone on board his train of music discovery. The dude LOVES music. He is a pure fan of music and talks about it all the time. He lives for nostalgia, and music is a huge part of the overall feeling of nostalgia. Music connects with you at different points in your life in meaningful ways that change you forever, and it seems like this usually occurs in high school and college. To this day, Joey has a sort of "back in the day" music taste sensibility. His connection and love for the underground music of the time proved to be beneficial to Emery. Joey knew about all the bands that the Greer crew did not.

Joey was from Charleston, South Carolina (a city much larger than the small town of Greer) and had an older brother with good music taste. This gave Joey the leg up on the other guys for discovering cool music. "My brother and I, we listened to the very very outlier Christian music," Joey boasted. "Bands guys like Aaron Sprinkle would know - 77's, The Choir. I would say we were pretty legit non-poser indie rockers. We would go to all the shows and stuff." It may come off as self congratulatory, but Joey is really intent on making it known that he cared deeply about seeking out unknown bands that he felt offered more substance than just what you might get on the radio. And honestly, he has a point. In the mid 90's, the Christian indie/punk scene was just emerging. There were no Relient K's and Underoath's making gold records. Brandon Ebel was just getting Tooth and Nail off the ground, paving the way for future success of those types of bands. But at the time, the only way to know about it was to go to the show, order records via a mail-order catalog, or hope that your local Christian bookstore was hip enough to carry a few punk records, which of course likely went against the bookstore owner's "better" judgment.

"When I met Toby, junior year of college, he was listening to R. Kelly. The only CD that he was really into that I loved was Foo Fighters. I let him listen to a lot of stuff I was listening to," Joey continued. "Some pop punk - Slick Shoes - but when I let him listen to the "Whole EP" [Pedro the Lion], it just blew his mind. Just literally he was like 'I cannot believe this'." Matt confirmed Pedro the Lion's influence as well.

At this point, Joey and Toby still didn't know Matt or Devin. It wasn't until their senior year of college that they started hanging with Matt and Devin regularly. "I would make Matt compilations," Joey said, and Joey's influence continued. It was trickle down indie music economics. Sunny Day Real Estate came into the picture. "There's no way you can listen to a disk like this and not be like, 'This is unreal,'" Joey exclaimed in reference to SDRE's 1998 release, "How It Feels to Be Something On". Joey was doing the Lord's work there in Rock Hill, SC, pulling these jokers up from the depths of R Kelly and Korn music hell.

Ironically, Toby didn't miss the opportunity to let his newfound love of indie and emo music pump up his ego, according to Joey. "Toby made a comment one time and I'll never forget. He said, 'Man I'm into the kind of music Matt and Devin is [sic] into, but I'm also into the more indie stuff that you like. I think that makes me better than all of y'all.' He was being serious." Joey and I shared a good laugh over that one.

The discovery of completely new forms of music outside of what you thought was possible is a revelation. It inspires you to create and push yourself to achieve greatness. Bands like Further Seems Forever and Jimmy Eat World did that for me. For Emery, Pedro the Lion was groundbreaking, and Joey was the one who introduced them to a new scene. So while his influence on Emery is sometimes questioned, Joey was instrumental in Emery discovering "good music".

*****

Tremont Music Hall in Charlotte, NC is just a half hour from Winthrop University. I've played there many, many times in my own band but never realized that the venue was instrumental in Emery's introduction to the indie/punk/hardcore scene. It was the closest venue to Winthrop that would put on those type of shows, and lucky for them, some pretty fucking cool bands would often perform.

Brandtson, Sunny Day Real Estate, Rising Tide,

Self Minded, Zao, Juliana Theory, Lutikriss (who would one day become Norma Jean) were all bands that came through during their college days. Hopesfall and Stretch Arm Strong, who were both from the area, were regulars as well.

As one might imagine, going to shows like these was a whole new world for the rednecks from Greer. "I'd seen people jump around on TV, like grunge jumping around, but this wasn't that," Matt explained. "We were so angry," Matt says of initial hardcore show experiences. "Toby was standing there like, 'What the fuck is this; little skinny person with hair and a bandana and they're dancin'...doing "ninja". It just made no sense at all."

Hardcore dancing is a culture shock everyone experiences the first time they see it. There is no frame of reference to compare it to. Ninjas doing Ninja-y stuff. That about sums it up. I'm with Toby on this one. If you aren't familiar with hardcore dancing, go look up AFI's video for 'The Leaving Song Pt. II'. That video will get you well acquainted with this style of dancing that is quite frankly, in my humble opinion, stupid. Matt and Toby are in agreement with me on this.

It goes without saying that they didn't quite fit into

this scene when they first happened upon it. I asked Matt about "fitting in". "I didn't think of anything as fitting in. It wasn't a matter of fitting in. I didn't think about fitting in or not fitting in. I didn't think about looks…at all. Not as it relates to music. I'm different than other people. I never thought about my looks, period. I don't think about that naturally. Of course we didn't fit in. We weren't trying to be a band. I'm sure we looked like old guys there [at the concerts]."

Were they preppy college dudes in polo shirts?

"Every clothes [sic] I wore was XXL." Matt responded. "It would be like your brother in law from somewhere in Arkansas who was 25 wound up at an Emery show. He would have no connection to what was going on."

Matt's assessment paints a perfect picture for someone who first happens upon the scene. At some point, everyone who went on to be a "player" in the scene was that brother in law that Matt is hypothetically referring too. Nobody comes out of the womb with tattoos, wearing girl jeans, and hardcore dancing all Ninja-like.

The first time I saw my band, As Cities Burn, play,

I was wearing a Tommy Hilfiger button-down and baggy jeans. It took me 10 seconds to dye my hair black once I joined a hardcore band. I like that it probably took awhile for Matt to shed his XXL wardrobe. There is an authenticity to that attitude that I wish I had.

So how do you get from XXL clothes and alternative radio rock to screamo legends? First they had to quit a couple of bands.

*****

"*Joe 747, they were* more like emo/indie and I remember thinking, 'Man I really like their sound way better than the band I was in'," Seth told me. "Definitely Emery's sounds came more out of Joe 747 than any other band that any of us were in." To say Seth was envious of Toby and Joey's band sounds like an understatement. It also could have something to do with the fact that he wasn't a part of it. Joey clarified the facts regarding the makeup of Joe 747. "Matt and Devin actually played in that band for the majority of our existence."

Based on Seth's description of the sound of Satchel - that was the name of Seth, Matt, and Devin's band in college - I can totally understand where his envy stems from. "Simply Waynes. That was our high school band, then that turned into some stupid name...Satchel. It's kind of Limp Bizkit, Tool sounding. What, nu metal?" I confirmed that yes, nu metal was the correct classification. You could also throw in the rap rock genre if they truly were taking influence from Limp Bizkit.

It's interesting getting the different perspectives from these guys as far as genre and influences of the time. Joey had a totally different memory of Satchel. "When Toby and I were doing Joe 747, that was the sound we were shooting for (90's emo). While Matt and Devin were playing the Helmet, Silverchair, Rage Against the Machine, we were playing this weird stuff. You know people would come to shows on our college campus and look at us like 'This is really good but I don't know if I get it'. Like, we would play a show and a couple people would walk out when I started screaming because this is the south its kind of like 'What are they doing?'."

This is when we get into Joey's value of nostalgia again. As Joey remembers it, Joe 747 was a great band and people just didn't get it at the time. This isn't to say that Joe 747 was bad. But Joey remembers it more fondly because, musically, he didn't do anything past that band really. I followed up with Matt once I had reviewed my interview with Joey. I was skeptical of the lack of objectivity that Joey viewed his college band. Matt had this to say, at length:

"When I say it's good, it's not really a good band at all. Like if they played before you at that club in Virginia Beach, you wouldn't have thought it was a good local band." Matt is referencing a venue on the strip in Virginia Beach, VA. As Cities Burn actually opened for a tour Emery was on, which why I suspect Matt brought up that example. He continued, "There were good indie bands at the time. They existed (but) there weren't bands that were tight. So they (Joe 747) looked terrible, and the sound was bad and the playing and the timing was bad," Matt said. "But still at the core of it, it had Toby singing and some really interesting chord progressions and melodies. But if you didn't know you couldn't be impressed by it. You wouldn't have been able to identify as being good."

Matt does give some credit to Joe 747 though, "Emery is Joe 747 plus other influences. It was just before it came across well." He went on, "Toby was just this actual real talent. 'Holy shit', it was just obvious. This is really catchy." Even with Toby as a diamond in the rough, Joe 747 had a long way to go in Matt's opinion. "We were so far off from any community, we didn't know what amps to use or what guitars or sounds, or how to dress or how to set up on stage. We weren't part of a scene, so there was not anything to copy or emulate. So the only thing we were emulating was sounds on records. The whole part of being a local band is you learn stuff. Stage presence, look, delivery, performance." As any new local band would be, Joe 747 was absent of all of these band skills.

Joey's optimism and lack of objectivity blocked him from realizing the truth behind these realities. "He would say stuff that wouldn't make any sense," Matt said. "Me and Devin listened to Deftones and Korn at the time. Joey would have told you that Joe 747 was better than Deftones and Korn. He probably would have told you that OUR band (Satchel) was better than Deftones and Korn." Satchel is the band that according to Seth was trying to *sound* like Deftones and Korn. "You would say, 'No! How can you say that?' And he would list a bunch

of reasons and say, 'Well, I guess I just don't get it?' He
is not aware of all the things that are coloring his bias. I
think he literally lacks that ability to think objectively,"
Matt said.

I explain to Matt that I'm not trying to shit on Joey
and his memory of Joe 747. But it's rare to have
someone reflect so favorably on what was essentially just
a local band. It's the same as if I thought my first ska
band was just so awesome. If I had never done anything
else, maybe I would have kept feeling that way. I guess it
seems like it would be like thinking my pop punk band,
freshman year was just awesome. But I might have
thought that had I never done anything else. It's like my
dad. He thinks for sure, that As Cities Burn is better than
Arcade Fire. "Arcade Fire is not a rock band. They are
not a rock band!" he once exclaimed to me while
watching their performance on SNL.

"Yeah it's like that," Matt said. "It's lack of
objectivity. Musically, Joey just doesn't have the
experience."

Matt and Devin's band (Satchel) and Toby and
Joey's band (Joe 747) had to join forces to become
Emery. According to Matt, Joe 747 was not technically a

"good" band. Joey's sense of nostalgia says otherwise. He believes they were a great band, but that people just "didn't get it" at the time. Like I said, Joey got all these guys into the music that would influence the future of Emery. Through that process, Joey and Toby actually humbled Matt and Devin. "I thought we understood music well," Matt said. "We, me and Devin, thought we were the veterans." Simply Waynes and Satchel had played a lot more shows than Joe 747. There was this sense in Matt's mind that he was doing a favor for Toby and Joey by agreeing to play for them. As noted earlier, Toby was the real talent, and Matt caught on quickly. "What we need to do is be serious with Joey, Toby, Matt and Devin. Take the people that really care. Just make one band" Matt said. This was after Matt and Devin had stopped playing for Joe 747 to focus on Satchel. But the move was obvious to both sides. Join forces, get serious, and move. Far away. Forget the girlfriends. Fuck getting real jobs. Fuck real life.

A top secret rendezvous at a Mexican restaurant would change lives and set the course for a string of events that would test friendships, future marriages, and the financial stability of wide-eyed dreamers with a lot to lose. College graduates don't do this shit. College graduates go to grad school, or get jobs. Or take over the profitable family business. Or settle down immediately and marry their hot ass college sweethearts and start popping out babies. It's incredibly stupid to view a band as a viable career. It's incredibly stupid to move to the literal opposite side of the country, with no plan whatsoever. What could have possibly been said at that Mexican restaurant in Rock Hill, SC. What drugs were cooked into the fucking delicious bowl of white cheese dip to cause a group of otherwise responsible, educated men to leave everything behind to chase a dream?

In reality, very little was said.

5

SETH THE ENTERTAINER

I was supposed to meet Seth at 11:00am for coffee at a Starbucks in Tukwilla, a suburb south of Seattle near the airport. As far as I could recall, I had never met Seth. He wasn't in the band when As Cities Burn toured with Emery in 2005 or 2007. My trip to Seattle had been a breeze thus far. I had met with Josh the night before to eat, drink, and interview. Josh let me crash on his floor in his tiny Capitol Hill apartment, and when I mentioned that I needed to make the 20 minute trek south to meet Seth the next morning, Josh offered up his van as a means of transportation. "I never even drive it," he said. Do you believe in omens?

I was going to take an Uber. I should have taken the Uber. It wasn't a matter of budget. I had the money to take an Uber. I flew all the way to fucking Seattle to interview Seth and the expense of a $20 Uber ride was not an obstacle at this time. I said yes to the van. I said yes to that fucking piece of shit van. Josh was just being nice. He is a nice guy, whatever that's worth. He mentioned the gas gauge didn't work but that I should be good to go on fuel. He recommended I put some fuel in the tank before I headed back from Tuckwilla just to be safe.

It was cold on this fateful morning. Cold and wet. A typical December morning, perfect for a meeting at Starbucks, which by the way is a local joint in Seattle. I support local business. I made it to the exit for Tukwilla in the piece of shit child molester van and as I am pulling off the interstate under an overpass I feel the steering wheel go stiff. The van shuts down and now I am cruising under the overpass with a shoulder about 2 feet wide. As I pull over I am still basically in the middle of the road. The van will not restart. Panic sets in. Fuck Fuck Fuck. I struggle badly with anxiety and being late to a meeting is about the worst thing I can imagining happening. Late to a meeting AND stranded on the side of the road in a brown child molester van is anxiety overload.

It would have been nice if this was one of the many thousands of interstate exits in this country that had a strategically placed gas station mere feet from the off ramp. Tukwilla has no such gas station. I believe it was a third of a mile to the nearest gas station with no sidewalk. Well out of sight of the van, this gas station was up and over a hill on the road leading towards the mall - the mall with the Starbucks.

It's raining, not too hard, but raining nonetheless. I am sporting somewhat fashionable boots with the soles having been worn down because I typically wear the same pair of shoes everyday until they fall apart and I get a new pair of shoes. I'm wearing jeans, a hoodie, a flannel, and a knitted red cap (like the one Bill Murray wore in "The Life Aquatic") none of which respond well to rain. I decide I have no choice but to run - the best I can in my hip boots - to the gas station, buy a gas can, and load up on some fuel. I left the hazards on in the van and set off.

With the gas station being over the hill and out of sight, I'm not going to be able to see what's going on back at the van. I'm very worried about it getting towed or worse, an inattentive driver plowing into it. I'm trying to run but I am a fat piece of shit. So out of shape that I can only make it about 100 yards per jogging attempt. My lungs are burning, my head is throbbing and now I'm sweating under my flannel and hoodie despite the fact that it's probably 39 degrees outside. I'm also slipping and sliding due to my fashion boots and the worn down soles because like I said, I've worn them every day for 2 or 4 years.

I get the gas can and the gas. I start fat running back to the van, slip and fall a few times, lungs basically collapsed. As I pass over the slight hill shielding my view of the van from the gas station, my stomach drops. Blue lights are flashing. Cop SUV is pulled up behind the van. The officer is kind of walking around it inspecting and wondering what the hell is going on. I start waving frantically. Fat running and waving. I hold up the gas can as if to signal to the cop my misfortune. I'm not sure what I was worried about happening. Yes the van had no windows on the side and was shady as fuck, but I'm sure the officer would be quite reasonable when I explained that I simply ran out of gas in a shit van with a broken fuel gauge. I don't think it's illegal to run out of gas.

Maybe my #whiteprivilege played in my favor with this encounter with the law, but the officer was very gracious and gave me no troubles. Apparently somebody that worked at city hall had called it in as they passed the van and at that point he was more concerned with keeping me safe from passing vehicles while I tried to refuel. Now I just had to get the fuel tank cap open. Easy enough right? Nope. This one uses a fucking key. I have a key chain with like 7 shitty old keys and none of them are working. I come real close to breaking one off in the gas cap. The officer gives it a try, to no avail. There was a trick to it where you had to push in while turning and eventually we figured it out. Gas cap off.

I had informed Seth via text by now that I had run out of fuel in Josh's shitty rape van and I would be a little late. Little did I know that I don't know how to operate a fucking gas can. I installed the spout incorrectly somehow. It isn't penetrating the fuel tank and instead I am just spilling gasoline all over my hands, fashion boots, hoodie, flannel and the road. This is a nightmare. The officer - bless his heart - tries to assist but he can't figure it out either. Since when did gas can get so god damn complicated? Every time I think I have penetrated - I'm really going to take advantage of using the word "penetrate" because I'm immature and sex - anyways every time I think I have PENETRATED the gas tank I continue to spill fuel all over my hands and fashion boots. Now I'm just going to smell like gasoline for the rest of the day because there is no washing that shit off. It has to wear off over the course of a few days. And I didn't even bring extra clothes on this trip. Was only planning to be in Seattle for two nights. One pair of jeans. One pair of shoes. One flannel and hoodie. Now with the distinct aroma of 87 octane fuel.

We could not get this fucker to work. No fuel was reaching the tank. It was all going straight to the road beneath us. The gas can was only 2 gallons and now at least 1 of those gallons was wasted. I finally took the spout apart and tried to reassemble. I couldn't even tell you specifically what I did right that time, but I made it work. If I had to do the same thing right now I wouldn't have a fucking clue. The Good Lord had intervened. That extra gallon of fuel that I spilled on the road would have really come in handy because the fuel I was able to get into the tank was not enough to start the van. The cop didn't look mad at me…he just looked disappointed. I explain that I will run back up to the gas station and have my "friend" Seth meet me there and drive me back so it won't take as long.

I call Seth to inform him of the plan. I apologize profusely. When he meets me at the gas station - myself covered in gasoline, reeking and flammable (hoping to avoid any open fires or cigarette smokers) - it will be the first time we have ever actually met. "Hi, I'm Aaron. I'm covered in gasoline. Can I ride in your car?"

It took every ounce we could get out of that can to start the van. I thanked the officer and instructed Seth to follow me to the gas station so I could put more fuel in then we would head over to our Starbucks rendezvous for what I assumed would be a shortened interview due to Seth's schedule for the day. But at least everything was good to go with Josh's creepy brown hide a body van. Except…

Now the van won't start. It's not the fuel. We have fuel now. It just won't fucking start. Seth gives it a try, pumping the gas and jiggling the steering wheel. It starts. Crisis avoided. I get as far as the exit of the gas station parking lot and the van dies again. I was following Seth and he didn't notice me not pulling out behind him so I have to call to inform him that I'm not moving. He doubles back and we spend the next 20 minutes looking under the hood (not sure what we were looking for as we both verbalized that we know nothing about cars) and attempting to turn this piece of shit over. We got nothing. My day keeps getting worse. What hell am I supposed to do with this van. I have shit to do. I need to interview Seth, then I need to eat ramen and then I'm meeting with a local food writer before I eventually meet up with Matt for dinner and his interview. And now I have a broke down van at a random gas station in Tukwilla, Washington. I call Josh to give him the rundown of all the problems. He tells me that the van "has never broken down before." I sure do have a way with automobiles. Actually this is all further proving the theory that my ex-mother in law was an advocate of - "Aaron, I think you have a black cloud following you everywhere you go."

I decide that my only option is to leave the van there. I have too much to do and too little time to do it. I didn't break Josh's van. It serves no logical purpose for me to sit around and wait for a tow truck or wait for Josh to get down there and try to fix it. I text Josh my decision because I'm a pussy and I don't do phone calls to tell someone something they may not want to hear. I know Josh and I know he won't fight me on it. Also non-confrontational. Still, I contend this is correct decision regardless. You gotta leave the van. Josh says he will figure something out. I'm so relieved to get in the car with Seth and drive to the Starbucks, leaving the piece of shit van behind at the gas station. I'm never borrowing a car from Josh again. You may be asking yourself why I have thus far spent almost two thousand words recounting this story. Well I think it's a funny story. I think it's a funny way to meet someone. And while this isn't Josh's chapter, I apologize for the sixteenth time for running out of gas, screwing up our interview time, and getting gas all over his upholstery, Seth leans over and says, "Dude don't worry about it. I'm not that surprised. That's just a typical Josh situation…unreliable."

*****

I really like Seth. Just on a basic level. Like I said, I didn't know him going into this AT ALL. I had asked Matt about him and he gets high marks from his band mates. Seth is funny, but not on purpose. It's a combination of him being really short, really southern, and really blunt. It's not a laughing *at* him type of thing. Just sometimes, he isn't meaning to be funny, but he is fucking hilarious. His wardrobe has adapted to the northwest lifestyle - flat billed hat, quintessential Northwest-style Northface puffy jacket.

He stuck around Seattle after leaving Emery. That was over a decade ago, and there is no indication that he would ever in a million years consider moving back to South Carolina. In my view, that is quite admirable to have the will to stay far away from "home" for that long. Seth has either found a way to tolerate all the bullshit that I can't stand about the Northwest - liberal, PC, disconnected, an asinine $15 per hour minimum wage - or he has simply become one of them.

If there was anybody in the band that I would argue just wasn't meant to be in a band, it would be Seth. Almost everything in my interview with Seth and in my discussions about Seth with the other band members point towards this conclusion. He was never particularly impressive behind the drum kit, something I feel awful saying as a fellow drummer. This is not some snobby drummer judgment on my part. I have plenty of quotes from various band members in reference to Seth's abilities on drums. The distinction is amplified by the fact that Dave - Seth's successor - is an absolutely unbelievable drummer. Dave IS a DRUMMER. Seth is the friend from the small town who learned how to play drums, and your band needs a drummer, so sure, sign him up. He was willing, and that counts for a lot. It's really difficult to get a bunch of kids on the same page with starting a band and risking it all. Seth was willing to do that.

Girls, man. Fucking girls plagued Seth from the outset. The two biggest obstacles for start-up bands are, "How the fuck are we going to eat?" and relationships. I usually tell people that are already married and have dreams of starting a band and going on tour to wake the fuck up. It's not happening, dude. If your wife didn't meet you on tour, knowing you from the outset as a man on the run, the chances of figuring out how to make that work are pretty much zero. In the case of my band, not one of the relationships that we were in when the band started lasted past the first year of touring. Eventually, you have to choose. Seth was almost out before it even started.

He actually wasn't on board to do the band full-time at first. Devin was going to be the drummer and Seth would stay in South Carolina. "I had a girlfriend for five years, so I'm not gonna give that up," Seth told me. He had a change of heart, but his first stint in Seattle only lasted about six weeks. The relationship with his long time girlfriend was not going well, or as he put it, "Stuff went crazy," and he returned home only for the relationship to end shortly thereafter.

"I came back, we broke up and I was like, 'Great, all my friends are gone. What am I gonna do?' I was depressed. I just literally sat on the couch for two days straight." Friendship prevailed as the guys felt really sorry for Seth and invited him back to Seattle to rejoin the band.

Even though Seth did stick around for a few years, he would struggle with the purpose of the whole thing. I gather that he did like hanging out with his friends, and maybe even enjoyed the work of being in a band. But the pursuit, the two-a-day practices, the scouring the internet for shows and making phone calls all day to clubs, the sending out demos to record labels, Seth just didn't have that in him. "Just everyday hittin' it hard. Just hustlin." I think drummers naturally gravitate towards these sorts of tasks. There is a feeling that you need to contribute in ways outside of the creative side of things, especially in the beginning. If your singer is in one room writing lyrics, and your guitarist is in another room tracking demos, you sure as hell better be trying to book a show or something.

It was something to do, even if he eventually didn't know what the hell he was doing. On the Tooth and Nail tour in the spring of 2004, Emery was hanging out at Denny's with mewithoutYou. Seth began to step outside of himself and realize the painful trivialness of it all. "I was just looking around and was like, 'What the hell am I doing? This sucks. I'm just eating food. I'm just talking to people.' It was draining for me." Seth swore to himself that he would never go to Denny's again.

I figure that a person either buys into the idea that being in a band is fun and a really cool job, and that's good enough. Or, they buy into some bigger mission of the band. This "bigger mission" could be religious or political or whatever. It could be to just make as much money as possible, a worthwhile mission if you ask me.

It's the difference between U2 and Blink 182. Change the world or make dick jokes. I guess a band can fall in between. Maybe Emery does. It's almost inevitable that if a band does start with a mission that the mission will slowly fade the longer they operate as a professional entity.

Before we get into the shitty side of Seth, I would like to offer up some disclaimers. Every "Christian band" hooks up with girls. Every "Christian band" has somebody that tries some drugs or uses drugs. Every "Christian band" has a drink or five. Now, of course Emery wouldn't call themselves a "Christian band" on the grounds that no such thing exists. But some of you reading might think Emery is a "Christian band". And before you continue I want to toss that bullshit term to fucking curb. It's not a real thing. It's a marketing tool. It's a way to identify a demographic and then sell to them. Emery is not above reproach. They are just like you, except got to do cooler shit, and had more girls and free beer available to them than normal people. So with that said, lets get down to the dirty stuff.

Seth might be an alcoholic. I asked him about a story that involved Cracker Barrel and a confrontation with Toby, and he couldn't remember it all. Josh and Toby both mentioned it in their interview and Seth had no recollection. "I quit drinking almost a year and one month ago, and I think I killed brain cells," he told me as 'Silent Night' played in the background.

He told me that nobody really drank in the early years. Now, having toured with Emery hundreds of days at this point in my life, I can fully attest that "nobody really drank" is a long gone reality at this point. Emery gets down. I could almost argue that Emery taught me how to drink. I don't mean that in a bad way either. In the heyday, if you were chillin' with Emery, IT WAS ON. And it was fun.

"It just creeps up on you," Seth elaborated. "You know, have a beer you gotta chill out. Then, damn, I was finding myself drinking pretty heavily every single day; drinking and driving."

"Are you an alcoholic?" I asked.

"I don't know." Seth went on, "At least three or four every single day. On the weekends, it was on. I would black out." He said he would forget where he parked the car. I don't know if that means 'THE CAR WAS IN THE FRONT YARD I CAME IN THROUGH

THE WINDOW!!!' (Lit anyone? Best band name by the way). "It was just something to do," he said nonchalantly. That's some truth. He told me that he would try to say he wouldn't drink before noon. "11:59 it's like, alright. And once you open that beer it's alright. I'm chill." A beer at noon is the chillest feeling in the world. It's really only something that band folks get to experience without seriously compromising their daily productivity. I remember in between shifts cooking at a restaurant in Louisiana I would go to a pizza joint and down a pitcher and then go back and finish my double. It sounded like a good idea, but about two hours into dinner service I'm chopping off finger nails as I try to slice a chicken breast.

Band life perpetuates this idea that drinking whenever is basically a right. When you are home from tour for three weeks, you sure as hell aren't getting a job. You are just home, so, when noon rolls around, it's time to party. It's the best. And Seth took full advantage of this lifestyle for the short time he was in the band.

When I asked him if he regretted quitting the band before they got REALLY big, he told me, "Oh, not really." That is a very telling detail about Seth. I envy the idea of having no regrets, especially when you see your buddies go on to do amazing things. When he was in the band, there were no hotels or tour buses. It was the van, every night. Maybe you'd crash on floors with people. He stated that his only regret was that he didn't get to go overseas with Emery (I didn't mention it, but going overseas with your band fucking sucks).

Seth knows that had he been in the band as they got bigger, he would have just gotten shittier. "I think I would have had a lot more sex and a lot more drinking." The opportunity certainly would have been there. "I never did drugs much, but it probably would have crept in there." Once again, the opportunity certainly would have presented itself.

Matt told me an absolutely fantastic story about Seth that occurred when they were still playing local shows around Seattle. "We played this show down there in Ballard (Seattle) at this place called the Ballard Firehouse." It was a battle of the bands but before the show, there was some sort of radio DJ event for this guy named Tom Leykes, one of those douchey, shock-jock local radio guys. "So everyone was pouring out of there, drunk people pouring out of the Tom Leykes event, and we didn't know where Seth was. There was [sic] girls there… slutty girls were taking their tops off, and we found Seth a few minutes later and he was signing girls' boobs. Grabbing the boobs and had a sharpie and was signing them." Matt is laughing his ass off telling this story. For the most part, Emery was a pretty straight-laced crew and didn't get into too much trouble. "Devin for instance was, like, devastated by seeing a boob. But Seth, he would do stuff he thought was bad, but couldn't help it.

"I was hooking up even in the small days. Well…I don't wanna…" He got real quiet. I'm not sure why because it's not like anybody at the Tukwilla, WA Starbucks had any idea who he was or who we were talking about. Also, we were "on the record" so I am basically free to write about whatever he tells me unless he expresses otherwise. But I love when I'm trying to get dirt and the person starts getting quiet. That means it's about to get good. "This is a really weird story. There were these two girls, and I don't know if you are gonna write about this because if they read it they would know who they were…"

Of course I'm going to write about this, you dirtbag. This is why I flew four thousand miles to interview you at a damn Starbucks. Seth whispers, "It was me, Devin, and Toby, and we all hooked up…we didn't have sex, just blowjobs and stuff." I'm pretty sure he didn't mean all together. Not like an orgy. "They were just groupies and that's all," he told me.

I asked if this was all the time, or a one-time thing? "Oh yeah, this is what we do, come on," Seth said. Emery did have a record deal at this point, after all. "This wasn't even touring life, that was just chicks that knew we were in a band because we dressed like we were in a band." The girls were plentiful. Again, I will stress that this is the case with every band - well the bands I know of anyways. It has nothing to do with Christian or not Christian. It has to do with guys having dicks and balls, and those dicks and balls want to be played with. For whatever reason, women are down with this. Don't ask me why.

"I felt like shit for years. Man, I was a shitty person."

*****

"Our van broke down in Montana." If you

have never been to Montana get your ass there ASAP. It's amazing and beautiful. I've driven across the state many times and I will never tire of it. Seth used to go on walks when Emery was on tour. Like if they broke down on the interstate or had a flat tire, he would just start walking and then the guys would pick him up down the road. This is a great idea by the way. Wish I had done it while the other assholes in my band had to change a flat tire. "I just started walking. 'You guys fix it, just pick me up.' I walked several miles down I-90. I was just thinking. I think I was praying out loud - Should I quit the band?" When the Emery van broke down that day in Big Sky Country, Seth left the van totally undecided about his future with Emery. By the time they picked him up? "Guys, I got something to tell you."

Seth was engaged when he decided to quit the band. His relationship with his now wife, Melanie, just wasn't working with the rigors of the band life. There is much more to that as they had serious problems even after he quit. He has gone into great detail about their marriage on the BadChristian podcast, but Emery was not the main culprit here. That relationship was fucked up, and it's a blessing and a miracle that they figured it out. Even after

Seth decided it was time to quit, he didn't leave the guys stranded without a drummer. He even cut his honeymoon short to make it back for a show. "We went to Hawaii for four days." I pointed out to Seth how fun and odd it was that he cut his honeymoon short for a band he was quitting, while Devin took an entire summer off after he got married at the peak of the band's popularity. "He was wiser than I was," Seth conceded.

Seth Studley is the guy that fits in perfectly with this group of people. If only he was a better drummer and had more self control, he might have stuck for the long haul. But it's clear to me that life as a band dude was just not his calling. If I didn't like Dave so much I might be bummed that Seth didn't stick around. Emery was a better band with Seth leaving. And Seth might have drank and fucked himself to death if he had stayed.

I think it all worked out for the better, and it makes me happy that Seth truly doesn't regret leaving. "It's not that big of a deal, 'cause if you take the whole Emery narrative, I'm only like a small chunk of it."

Seth Studley currently resides in Seattle with his wife and children, and works as a counselor. I think by leaving Emery when he did, he is a much better person for it and I envy him in some ways that he was spared from experiencing any more time as a band dude. I assume he hasn't gotten any better at drums.

After our meeting, I took an Uber back to Seattle and ate ramen.

6

JOEY QUITS

Reason number 3,786 to love hanging with the Emery dudes? They know how to get down with Southern-style Mexican food. We eat at these kinds of places on pretty much every tour I've been on with them. Well, it's bastardized Mexican food, really. Think white cheese dip, unlimited tortilla chips, red sauce on everything, the tacos are hard shell and filled with ground beef unless you say otherwise. It's a weird understanding we southerners share with regards to this Mexican food. But there are few things on earth better than that white cheese dip. I drink that shit.

It wasn't until I started my research for this book

that I came to know the significance of the very type of Mexican Restaurant I have been rambling about. El Cancun, a name shared by dozens of other Mexican restaurants with identical menus, but in no way affiliated with each other, is ground zero for Emery. A discreet meeting, betrayal of friends, lack of consideration for relationships, and a plan to make a run for it make this worthy of my compelling screenplay seen below.

"Meeting at El Cancun Mexican Restaurant: The Story of Forming Emery"

based on a true story

FADE IN

INT. JOEY AND TOBY'S HOUSE - EVENING

JOEY (24) and TOBY (20's) are in the kitchen, JOEY sitting at the table and TOBY pacing franticly. TOBY is holding a "Zack Morris" style cellphone as JOEY intensely studies a map of the United States.

TOBY turns to JOEY and holds the cell phone up with his fingers on the dial button, as if threatening to make a phone call.

TOBY (thick southern accent)
I'm gonna to do it. I'm just going to call them right now and make them come meet us. I know they will say yes.

JOEY (thick southern accent)
Yeah, but you gotta tell them not to bring the other two idiots in their band. Make something up for why we are meeting.

TOBY
Ok, yeah that's a good idea, Joey. Man, I really like your ideas, Joey. Especially this band idea. You are really awesome.

TOBY and JOEY high five and hug.

TOBY
Where should we ask them to meet?

JOEY

Man, I could really go for some free chips and salsa, and white cheese dip. How about El Cancun?

TOBY

Shit dude! You are just a good idea factory. Ok, I'm gonna call Devin.

TOBY dials a phone number and waits for a connection, checking his watch and scratching his fat balls in the meantime.

TOBY

Hey…Devin. Yeah, it's Toby, your good friend. Hey, come meet me and Joey at El Cancun in 30 minutes….Yeah, but only bring Matt, and don't tell anyone else at the house what you are doing…Oh yeah, we just want to talk about…about…uh…

TOBY looks at JOEY seeking assistance for coming up with a lie. JOEY stands up and pretends to jerk himself off.

TOBY

…Oh yeah! we want to talk about starting an intramural
softball team…Yep, we just think that would be fun, but
seriously, ONLY BRING MATT…OK…Bye.

*JOEY runs over to TOBY with a hopeful look on his face,
dying to know what DEVIN's answer was.*

JOEY

Well? What did he say????!!!!

*TOBY lowers his head and acts sad. Like a puppy. A sad
puppy.*

TOBY

Well…I'm sorry Joey…but…THEY ARE GOING TO
MEET US AT EL CANCUN IN THIRTY MINUTES!!!!

JOEY

YIPPEEEEE!!!!!

INT. EL CANCUN MEXICAN RESTAURANT - NIGHT

TOBY, JOEY, DEVIN (early 20's) and MATT (age unidentifiable) are all sitting at a booth together. A short, spiky-haired Latino WAITER (20's) arrives with chips and salsa, and tall, red, plastic glasses of water for each of the guys.

WAITER (thick Latino accent)

Is there anything I can get you to drink other than water? Cerveza? Margarita?

DEVIN (thick southern accent)

Oh, actually sir, we are Christians. Sweet tea is fine.

TOBY

Fuck that. Get my ass a beer. The big one.

DEVIN is visibly disappointed in TOBY's choice to sin.

DEVIN

Toby, that's not a good witness. We are in public for God's sake!

Cut to TOBY downing entire beer in one gulp.

TOBY

Ahhhhhh, ok guys so we didn't ask you here to talk about
a softball team.

MATT (thick southern accent)
Well, I figured as much. What's the deal?

TOBY and JOEY look at each other with anticipation,
and nod to each other.

JOEY

Here's what we want to do. We want to start a new band
with you guys. That way, we don't have to kick out the
current members of both our bands. We will just start a
new band completely. New name and everything.

DEVIN
Ok, that could be cool.

MATT
Yeah, these other dudes we are playing with suck
anyways.

JOEY

Ok yeah, but here is the big part of the plan. Once everyone graduates college, we are just going to MOVE somewhere and try and get the band going.

MATT

Ok, I'm down.

DEVIN

Yeah that sounds good.

TOBY

Wait, that's it? No deliberation or questions? You are just saying yes?

MATT

Yeah, sure, why not? What else am I going to do?

DEVIN

Where we moving?

WAITER returns to table with another beer for TOBY.

WAITER

Do you gringos know what you would like to eat?

MATT

I'll have a Speedy Gonzales.

DEVIN

Yeah, I'll taaaake, the number 22. Beef.

TOBY

I'm just drinking, thanks.

JOEY

I would love a bucket of chips and a gallon of the white cheese dip please…Ok, so, yeah, where're we moving? We could go to…Jacksonville?

TOBY

Florida?

JOEY

Sure. Kind of close. Could go to the beach.

TOBY

Wow, that's real adventurous, Joey. I take back what I
said about your ideas you piece of shit. How about
Chicago?

DEVIN

Or maybe…Texas?

MATT

Or, we could go to…Seattle.

TOBY

Oooohhh. Seattle. That's sounds cool

JOEY

Has anyone ever been to Seattle?

MATT

Nope.

TOBY

No.

DEVIN

No. But I'll move there.

JOEY

Ok. So it's Seattle.

MATT

Alright, let's do it.

TOBY

Ok. Moving to Seattle.

JOEY, TOBY, MATT, and DEVIN all put there hands in the middle of the table.

ALL

One! Two! Three! SEEEEAAAAATTTTLLLLEEEE!

The WAITER arrives with JOEY's gallon of cheese dip, which TOBY proceeds to dump on everybody's head for a delicious and creamy celebration. Everybody then runs outside the restaurant without paying.

EXT. PARKING LOT - NIGHT

TOBY, JOEY, MATT and DEVIN start pushing each other into the bushes.

FIN

I'd say my chances of receiving the coveted Razzie award for this screenplay are good.

The decision to start this new band was quick. "Within twelve minutes of when we sat down at the Mexican restaurant, we had all said we were going to leave everything, and everybody, we ever knew and move up to Seattle and start a band," Matt said. "It wasn't dramatic."

Devin had other plans before this meeting, "If that conversation never happened, I would have maybe gone to grad school. Become a music teacher or something like that." There is actually a little bit of a discrepancy in the way this part of the story is recalled by different members of the band. Whereas Matt believes the decision to move to Seattle was made while meeting at the restaurant, Joey takes credit for coming up with that part of the idea before Toby even made the call to set up the rendezvous. According to Joey it went down like this. "We're going to Seattle. And hopefully you guys wanna come too, but that means ya'll have to leave your band behind and break that up. But we want you to come with us." Either way, the decision was made.

Joey, Toby, Matt, and Devin were moving to Seattle to start a band. To be clear, at this point, Seth and Chopper weren't in the picture as far as the band was concerned. They were actually both going to move with them just for fun, but not to start a band. Devin was going to play drums and Joey would play bass. Matt would play guitar and Toby would sing. That was the band. The worst question you could possibly ask a band in an interview is, "How did you get your band name?" But I actually do have a little info to dish out on that. Not the meaning behind the name, because who gives a shit. But, there were three bands name that were "finalists" in a sense.

"We loaded up like two sheets full of names for bands. I mean we literally had over a hundred." Joey said. "The top names were Emery, The Reginald, and

Same Day Forever. Matt came up with Same Day Forever, and I think I came up with The Reginald." Fortunately, in my opinion anyway, they went with Toby's name. Emery.

*****

Anybody that follows Emery knows Joey

was never really a part of Emery. So what happened? Why didn't he go to Seattle?

Joey and I are sitting in the office of the mega church where he works. This office is inside a tapas bar, a few miles west of downtown Charleston. He is a campus pastor for the Sea Island branch of Seacoast Church, a multi campus mega church based in Charleston. I don't really know Joey that well. I've listened to the BadChristian podcast, but that's entertainment and only allows me to know Joey as well as any "fan" of the podcast might. Of course the Emery dudes have been talking about him for years, and I've hung out with him on a few different occasions.

Much to my delight, Joey asks if I want to step into the bar to grab a beer before we start our interview. I oblige - duh - and I even pay for the beers seeing as how I have negotiated myself an expense account with BC Words (publisher). Essentially Joey is paying 1/3 of the bill since he is a 1/3 owner of BC Words, but that is neither here nor there. Joey tells me he officially played only one show with Emery. But as we've said before, Joey greatly influenced the Emery guys' musical awakening in college. He's important to this story. Starting Emery and moving to Seattle, "...was basically Joey's idea," Devin told me. "Well, we are going to Seattle and gonna be in a band," Matt said of the plan Joey effectively sold them on, "then Joey didn't go. He quit way before we ever started." Would you believe that Joey quit the band by writing a letter to Toby?

So why did Joey bail? Was it really girl problems? Kind of.

"This is where everything in me doesn't want to spiritualize it. But I can't see any other way, that this isn't all spiritual." Joey begins to explain. "That rubs Matt and Toby the wrong way because for them it's like, 'Why don't you own some of this?' I will say that what was going on inside was very spiritual, but then I wasn't carrying it out right."

According to Joey, leaving Emery involved an act of God. Matt and Toby seem to think that's a copout. "I will own the fact that I played it out wrong." Joey says. "It's just so bizarre that I am so excited about moving to Seattle, and then all of a sudden that drive and passion is just gone. It was early or late spring 2001, and we were playing shows and stuff, and I was like, 'I don't think I like this anymore. What in the world is wrong with me?' I was in Greer practicing. All of us talking about going to Seattle." Joey told me he was explicitly thinking during these practices that he was sure he wasn't going to Seattle. This was the middle of summer, about a month or so before they planned to leave town.

"I actually left [Greer] to go back to Charleston and I didn't even tell them. I was leaving practice and they were like, 'Next time we see you, we are going to be on the road going to Seattle,' and in my head I was like…no we're not." Joey had other plans. He wanted to get married.

"But, I dropped out of the band when this girl, who is now my wife said, 'I don't want to get married and if that's what your aim is, then we are through. I don't want anything serious to happen.' In fact, when I told her

I was not going to Seattle, she was like 'that sucks' because in her mind, her plan was she's gonna go to Southern California and do a life there. I was going to go to Seattle and do my life there we would keep in touch somewhat casually." Joey's future wife, Priscilla, thought there was a plan in place. She thought that Joey was taking a risk and doing something crazy. I have to believe that was attractive to her, and at the same time made her not feel as bad about leaving to pursue her dreams. Joey didn't know it at the time, but Priscilla had secretly thought they would probably get married. She wanted to have a life outside of the idea of getting married. and pursue "10 years of singleness," as Joey puts it. She wanted to have an adventure on her own. And Joey's plan to go to Seattle and pursue music allowed her to do that without a guilty conscious.

Joey continues, "Priscilla comes and visits during the summer, and I tell her, and I even show her, the letter. The infamous letter that I was going to send Toby. She was very upset."

"Were y'all in love at that point?" I ask.

"We were, but like I said, her mind was dead set against [marriage]," Joey responds. Joey recalls a key moment after Priscilla's summer visit. "I'll never forget when I dropped her off at the airport and we weren't any further along in the process of, 'Hey let's get engaged. Let's live in the same town,' or any of that stuff. The girl that I want to marry has no interest in getting married." Brutal. The idea of being in love, but the other person having no intention of taking it any further at that time. But wouldn't this make the Seattle move easier?

Joey admits, "The second-best thing for me to do would be to hang out with my best friends in Seattle, and not only am I not supposed to do that, but I don't even think I have that desire. I'm screwed. This sucks." Joey says. "Like, what am I gonna do? Teach for the third time in my hometown living with my parents? This just sucks." Joey had already been out of school and working as a middle school math teacher. Moving to Seattle to start a band at this point is way crazier an idea for him than Matt and Devin, who were still in college. But again, it was his idea.

"He's very big on, 'God called me to do this, not this' with everything," Matt told me. Once you get Joey talking about his dreams, and I mean his *actual* dreams, prior to quitting Emery, Matt's observation becomes apparent.

"I don't know what it was in my head. Here's where I can't help but to spiritualize it. I can't help but sound ridiculous. About a year and half prior [to quitting Emery], I had a dream of stuff that would unfold, and the dream was very random, and I even forgot about it." Joey recalls. "God brought the dream back to my mind, and I translated the dream and what God was trying to tell me. I'm not the dude that says these things happen all the time. This is the only time something this crazy has ever happened to me, so I wrote down everything. I realized, 'Shit, this is how my wife and I are going to get together. I don't need to worry about this.'"

Joey dropped Priscilla off at the airport convinced that they will be together, and also knowing there is no way he is going to Seattle. He had already mailed the letter explaining that he was quitting Emery to Toby's dad's house. After he left the airport, Joey started driving up the East Coast. Around this time, Toby received the letter from Joey. "I just said things along the lines of, 'I know I'm not supposed to do this.' Probably super spiritual...the desire is gone. I know I said this because we've joked around about it since, but I did a 'P.S. I'm rooting for you guys' at the end of the letter."

There is a pretty strong consensus that Toby was really upset about this development. Joey says, "when Toby got [the letter], he was devastated, and he called my mom. This was before cell phones. He can't text me or anything, so he calls my landline. My mom answers the phone."

Toby told Joey's mom that he got a letter from Joey saying he was quitting the band. All Joey's mom was able to tell Toby was, "He went north."

North. He went north. Joey dropped Priscilla off at the airport in Charleston and just hopped on I-95 and headed north.

"Well this sucks. I'm leaving," Joey recalls of his thinking at the time. "I'm leaving Charleston and I'm driving up the East Coast and we will see what happens." Joey ended up in Boston. He found himself wandering around the city looking for jobs. His only plan was to pursue what could only be described as a boyhood dream. "I thought maybe I could find the Boston Garden headquarters and I could just be a ball boy…for the Celtics."

When Joey finally called to check in with his mom,

she informed him that his brother, Jared, was vacationing in New Hampshire only a couple hours away from Boston. Joey drove out to see him, thinking it would be good to spend time with family. He confided in his brother what was going on with Priscilla, the band, and randomly leaving South Carolina to try and get a job with the Celtics.

If any of you can remember, people didn't tend to check their email every 5 minutes back in 2001, especially if you were traveling. So once Joey was settled in New Hampshire and had a heart to heart with his brother, he got around to checking his email. Priscilla had been frantically trying to get in touch with him. "Priscilla found out what I was doing through my mom, and at first she was kind of excited, but then she was just like, 'I hate this. I hate not knowing what's in your mind. I hate this because it feels like we're separate. Please email me. Please call me. This is driving me crazy.' [Priscilla] went through a complete mental shift." Receiving an email like that gets a boy's heart racing. To be wanted and desired by someone is at the very core of our human existence. Joey's situation had become an alternate storyline from 'Love Actually'.

Joey goes into more detail about the previously mentioned dream. "Part of that dream was that I would take a super long hike. It would be very strenuous. Which is exactly what I did. I drove nonstop...I did not sleep or anything. So, it was a very strenuous hike. And then in the dream, where I would end up is completely different than where I thought I would end up. So I'm climbing up a mountain thinking I would end up in this country and someone said, 'You know you're in a totally different country?' That sounds super bizarre, but basically I thought the trip up the East Coast was for my sanity. For me to figure things out." I'm skeptical of dream interpretation. But given the circumstances, I feel I must take Joey at his word. "Priscilla can even tell you to this day, it's unexplainable, but when I started doing that, she freaked out and thought, 'I gotta be with this guy.' The next thing in the dream was, 'You went to get her.' So here I am, talking to her in New Hampshire and I'm like, 'I'm coming to Iowa'. I drove all the way to Iowa. I didn't stop."

Priscilla was originally from Iowa. She met Joey at Winthrop. Just in case you were confused why Joey was driving to Iowa to see her.

"I get there and we're talking and I was just like, 'What is going on. What are you thinking?' And [she] was like, 'Well, I definitely wanna be with you. I wanna get married.' And I asked her when."

Priscilla responded, "I don't wanna wait long."

This is cliche as fuck…but dreams do come true, I guess?

*****

"Seth and I were in Costa Rica," Matt recalled. "My aunt lives down there, so we were down there to go surfing." Meanwhile, Toby received Joey's letter declaring his intentions to quit Emery. Matt continued, "I get back and I'm like, 'Well Ok. We'll get Joel and we'll do this.' I don't even remember feeling very emotional that we lost Joey." In Matt's mind, it was just a matter of replacing Joey. Not that he didn't value his friendship, but there was no reason that Joey losing his mind and quitting should keep Matt from pursuing music. "Joey wasn't anything, musically. It would have been great and everything, but at the same time, Joey was somebody who was semi-unstable."

I asked Devin, "Was Joey a good musician?"

"Not really, no." Devin replied.

Joey has openly admitted that he sucked at bass, so the harshness of Matt and Devin's criticism is somewhat softened by Joey's absolute acknowledgement. Joey had only bought a bass just to be in a band with Toby anyways. In Joe 747, Toby had to tell Joey what bass parts to play.

But then there was also the mental aspect. Matt had plenty to say in this regard. "Joey would have been a disaster…as somebody to live with; somebody to be around all day every day; to be dependent on. He's introvert. He's depressed. He's a downer. He's ultra cautious. All things that would have been a disaster. He's not good at bass, either. That would have been the least of the bad things about Joey."

Joey isn't oblivious to all of these concerns regarding his mental and musical shortcomings. Joey talked to me more about his reason for leaving and how Toby felt about it. "I do think the ultimate purpose of me leaving Emery was I was supposed to start a life with this girl, pretty much right away. I've heard Toby say things along the lines of, 'You could have gotten married to her

5 years later.' But I think as time went by, he realized in his mind there's no way I could have survived the tour life."

Regret is a bitch. Regret can make you miserable for the rest of your life - not finishing school, breaking up with a girl, every year that goes by without meeting your goals of losing weight, or not pursuing a dream. It's a crippling idea, regret.

"Y'all were blowing up, selling hundreds of thousands of records and all that. Was Joey ever like oh...fuck?" I asked Matt.

Matt quickly replied. "I don't think so."

Joey confirmed Matt's thoughts. Kind of. "So you don't have any regrets?" I asked. Joey, sighed and then took his time answering, as if to be careful.

"Some of my worst depression was from '98 to 2003, after we got married." Joey told me. "There was [sic] a solid two years that I didn't regret getting married, but I wished like anything that I could be married *and* be in the band." I believed him. You can tell when a man isn't happily married. As someone who has been in an unhappy marriage, I've experienced it first hand and can see it in others. But Joey loves his wife and I can tell he does not regret his choice to be with her. But when it comes to quitting the band, I think it's safe to say there is plenty to be desired for Joey in that sense. He did have *some* feelings of missing out.

"I thought I could be on the road hanging out with my friends and not be a school teacher; not having to do all these grown up things. Devin probably doesn't remember this, but I remember telling him something along the lines of 'I really wish I could join you guys and be back in the band.' I think there was a part of me that hoped he would say, 'Yeah, let's figure it out.'" This was after 'Weak's End' had come out in 2004 and things were starting to pick up for Emery.

"I can promise you this, it had nothing to do with 'Ooh now they're successful so I want back in.'" Joey just missed his friends. He talked about being in tears thinking about not being around the guys on this incredible journey. He loved his wife, yet he bailed on an adventure. It had to be difficult to want two things that seemed to conflict. Maybe regret is too a strong word to use in the case of Joey Svendsen. To this day, he truly believes this was all a calling, a divine intervention if you will.

"It was a hybrid of regretting it, but also knowing deep down inside that I did the right thing." This is a peace of mind that I envy. It makes me happy to see a man living what we band people would consider a "normal life" and be okay with it, even though Joey had the opportunity to take a different path. A path that would have led to touring the world, and playing in front of a thousand people every night, two hundred nights a year for almost a decade. I am glad for Joey that he can see it for what it's worth; to believe that band life just wasn't meant to be. That is incredibly valuable to his sanity. Ironically, sanity is something he lacks. As I've gotten to know Joey and learn more about his battle with depression (see Joey's book 'Fundamentalist' for a comprehensive and insane account of his mental illness), I'm confident that he would not have been able to handle touring. For all the lack of responsibility, touring is mentally difficult. Touring has taken a toll on me, without a doubt: my social development, my sense of responsibility, and my difficulty settling down in one place. Every week I am trying to convince my wife of some new place we should move to.

Joey's mental issues most likely would have

compounded on the road. Hell, maybe he would have destroyed his friendship with the guys in Emery, and BadChristian might never have happened.

Toby was devastated and angry at Joey's decision. He thought he and his best friend were going to go on an adventure together. Then his best friend pussed out over a girl. But looking back, everybody in Emery knows it was for the best. Joey, in his pride, is still optimistic about how he may have handled rock and roll fame.

"Do you agree with Toby saying you wouldn't have fared well on the road?" I asked Joey. He replied, "I think I'll be the first one to say that he very well could be right. But I also think I haven't experienced the road enough to know whether or not that would be true," Joey said. "I almost wanna disagree. But that's probably more of my pride talking."

Pride indeed.

Once the dust settled from the drama surrounding Joey's departure from Emery, it was decided that the band would continue on without him. Chopper would take his place as the bassist. Seth would be tagging along just for the hell of it, with no plans to be a member of Emery. The date for departure to Seattle was set.

7

THE GOLDEN CHILD

Devin can fucking whistle. Whistling skills may not seem impressive, but I would give anything to have access to a video of the whistling contest that occurred in the back lounge of the Emery bus early in 2008. As Cities Burn was sharing a really nice real-deal tour bus with Emery for their headliner that featured Mayday Parade, As Cities Burn, and Pierce the Veil. I need to be able to prove to you how incredible Devin's whistling performance of the theme song for "Legends of the Fall" was. That was his final round song choice. I don't remember who else had entered in the contest, but I do remember I was a judge, if not the sole judge. I had consumed many beers, which was the norm on that tour. Matt is not a singer so I was amazed he could whistle pretty damn well. In fact, he made it to the finals. However, no one can whistle like Devin.

Looking back, it's not surprising that Devin picked a movie theme song to clinch his whistling championship. The dude loves movies. When there was a day off on the tour, Devin always went to the movies. When I was tour managing Emery, I remember Devin would ever so politely ask if I wouldn't mind making sure the bus parked near a movie theater. I always found it endearing anytime Devin asked for something. He was so damn polite about it, but also calculating. Devin is easy to manage since he never asks for much, and his requests were easy to fulfill. "Hey Aaron, you think we could make sure and have some Diet Coke stocked in the cooler?" Sure thing, Devin! "Aaron, man I would love to get some Corona today. Maybe Corona Light, if they have it? Just any Mexican light beer would be fine." Your wish is my command, Golden Child.

Matt Carter was the first to make me aware that Devin is "The Golden Child" of his family. "Devin IS the golden child. First person in his family that ever went to college; [the] only person that doesn't live close by; amazingly athletic; great looking; could sing from the age of three in church. It's like in a movie, or that Mickey Mouse cartoon where the land is ravaged and there's the one golden calf or something. It's just the most special thing to his family."

Devin's family grew up poor and almost like a caricature of rednecks, as unfair as that may be. I say that in the way that somebody not from the South - say a 'tolerant' hipster from Seattle - would make judgments based on stereotypes that aren't accurate. Being a redneck doesn't equate to being dumb. Devin's family ain't dumb. "Some of his siblings are 'redneck rich' now," Matt told me. "All you would have to ever do is spend thirty minutes and meet all of Devin's family members, and your mind would blow, and you would understand everything that you would ever need to know about Devin."

I'm only now realizing how incredibly stupid it was to not go to Greer, SC and meet Devin's family. Everyone in the band reports they are amazingly nice and lovely people. Devin is an amazingly nice and lovely person, so it's not surprising to me. As Matt put it,

"They're not bad rednecks."

Dave said he genuinely has never understood a single word that Devin's dad has said to him. Apparently that's because Mr. Shelton almost exclusively speaks in sayings and phrases. I'm picturing Chris Farley's dad in "Tommy Boy" right now but instead of a Midwestern auto parts tycoon, more like '*Slingblade*' without the intellectual disability.

Devin's humble beginnings and good family life, combined with the fact that he seemingly got the good looking gene in the Shelton family DNA pool, set him up to be a smart, accomplished, and decent human being. He's the only member of Emery with whom I would feel a little bad if I were around him while drunk. It's not that Devin was ever judgmental. He would mostly just laugh at us. Devin didn't operate separately from the core of the group, just on a different wavelength.

When Devin left the band a few years ago, the business had just started to change and the dynamic of how the band operated was going through a transformation. He had gotten to the point where he didn't care for tour at all. He liked being around his friends. But he could take or leave the touring, and he eventually decided to leave it.

"Devin was less and less the hangout guy," said Matt, with a tinge of sadness in his voice. About the time leading up to Devin's departure, Matt said, "We probably got…not distant…as the band became more of a machine, being on tour was way less about that. We weren't writing in the same room. Then the dynamic of hanging out and having fun…he was just less and less goofy. It used to be Seth and Devin and Toby just cuttin' up."

The worst thing anybody can say about Devin is that he lacks ambition. It's not laziness. Devin is reliable, hard working, talented, and dedicated to the things to which he dedicates himself. But he is *content*, for the most part. He met a girl and fell in love and got married. He left big city life in Seattle behind and moved to her town in Illinois.

I visited his house to interview him. It's huge with an amazing basement that has a big movie screen and movie posters adorning the walls. It's a great house in the middle of nowhere. And Devin is totally OK with that. He works at a relatively large church in Champaign, IL, which is the closest "city" to his town – and he is OK with that. "Don't get me wrong, working at a church is great. Sometimes I feel a little bit silly. Growing up I never thought I would work at a church." He went on to explain that his "feeling silly" about working at a church comes from spending so much time in this legit kind of rock star world, and now he's trying to put together a worship band in a small city on Sunday mornings.

I asked Devin if he has 'what the hell is everyone doing' moments at his church job?

Devin laughed and answered carefully, but genuinely. "It's a weird dynamic. It's kind of hard...there is nothing necessarily better about one thing or the other. But nobody there understands the world I was in. That world still feels more comfortable 'cause I was in it longer." But Devin remains content. He doesn't want to be fifty years old chasing down a music dream. Actually, I don't think Devin would even want to be a successful fifty-year old rock star. He likes his family. He likes his little life in Illinois where he can play golf and live well. His wife is a wicked smart nurse practitioner. They do well for themselves and money goes a long way in the middle of the country surrounded by corn fields. They have two great kids, a basement with a ton of DVD's, and a basement bedroom turned into Devin's own personal music studio.

Devin sings like he could be in Boys II Men. That means that he sings like a black dude. He has soul combined with incredible vocal range. I think he could do just about anything he wanted to do in music. He told me that he submitted songs for Nashville studio gigs for awhile but nothing came of it, so he gave it up. I suggested to him that if he wanted to he could move to Nashville and make a career for himself as a songwriter and musician.

"Do I really wanna take more risks in my life? Or, just sit back and do what I'm doing." One would think this an incredibly depressing statement from Devin, but his tone when he said it was just very matter of fact. He has a family. He likes his life. It would be great if he could write songs and make a lot of money, but he doesn't *need* it. Devin's contentedness is enviable.

"I gotta be honest with myself. I'm a good musician, but I'm not a Nashville musician. I'm a singer first. My personality is like, be good enough to do what you need to do. I don't really care about mastering anything." It's an incredibly frustrating thing to hear from a guy who could do whatever he wants, but what he wants he has already achieved.

There is only a slight restlessness to Devin's demeanor that came off during the interview. I think it mostly has to do with what he was saying about working at the church. I got the he still slightly desires that feeling of really making and performing music in front of paying crowds.

Emery's way of going about things did change tremendously after Devin first left. At the time of his departure, Emery was still in a 'you're either in or you're out' mindset. It wasn't an ultimatum, but Emery was still on a very busy touring schedule. They were on the downside from the peak of their success, and maybe were thinking they could still make a "comeback" of sorts. But the comeback never really happened. Instead, they figured out a sustainable business model that allowed Devin to pop back into the mix. He helped write and record their last record, and has been playing shows with them pretty frequently over the past year.

"I've talked to Megan about it. Honestly, I don't really miss, like, traveling and all that stuff, you know? Being gone here and there a little bit is fine. I like being home." He did explicitly say he doesn't like not being involved in what's going on. I get the feeling that he feels left out. Not maliciously, but just by circumstance. He misses his friends. Even after he left, it has kind of felt like an open invitation to return and participate in any way he saw fit when he had time.

Emery is a better band when Devin is involved. The creative elements he brings to the writing process and the contrast of his vocal range to Toby's adds a dynamic that was missed during his hiatus. He's a genuinely good person, and a little dose of morality isn't such a bad thing to have in the Emery camp. Matt summed it up, "The opposite of coming from privilege and being shitty. What a wonderful way to be."

The Golden Child theory extends well beyond his family life. In Emery he is the best athlete, nicest person, has the best smile, he is the most all around talented musician, and he doesn't drink seventeen beers a day. Hell, he even gave me a bonus at the end of my first tour working for Emery. I am almost certain that Matt and Toby were highly opposed to that bonus. But Devin insisted that he felt it was the right thing to do. Devin was the only member of Emery in that "meeting" where I got that extra three hundred dollars. Devin is the GOAT.

8

2,736 MILES FOR A DAMN STARBUCKS

The waitress came bursting out of the kitchen to alert the members of Emery of the ongoing attacks in New York City by shouting,

This can't be right, Seth thought. "Tourists? What do you mean, like, people visiting New York?" Seth replied.

Devin interjected, "Oh, you mean terrorists…" The waitress came back with more info. "It was the son of Bin Laden."

But the story kept getting more confused. It seemed

like a Saturday Night Live parody for a character on Weekend Update. But this was very real. "We were like, *who is the Son of Bin Laden*?" I don't want to knock too hard on Cracker Barrel - it is a fine and hospitable food establishment if you happen to be on an Interstate - but to say I'm surprised at the lack of comprehension by the waitress of what was happening would be a lie. The members of Emery were on their way to Seattle, and probably somewhere in north Georgia or east Tennessee depending on what route they took. In other words, they pulled off in a town that probably doesn't fall too far from the redneck tree that Greer grew on. That means that the chance of a waitress at a chain country store believing that "tourists" and the "son of Bin Laden" were responsible for the attacks on 9/11 isn't outlandish. Sometimes, stereotypes are true.

Of course we all know what really happened that morning. The tourists were terrorists. The son of Bin Laden was Osama Bin Laden. Planes were hijacked and people were killed. The world changed in an awful way that day. No, I'm not going to insert a joke about Emery here. I'm serious. Even I can be serious about some things.

"What are your thoughts on it? You think it was an inside job?" Chopper posed this question to me during our phone interview. "I've read a lot of stuff on the internet. You hear a lot of fishy stuff about the guy taking out a gigantic insurance policy on the two buildings right before it happened." I never took Chopper as conspiracy theory type of guy. I certainly did not expect the conversation to head in this direction when I asked him what it was like to uproot his entire life on the same day as a terrorist attack.

I mean, *what a day* to choose to leave everything you know and venture into the unknown. 9 fucking 11. Talk about stealing a band's thunder. Al Qaeda wasn't going to let Emery have the spotlight. 9/11 can never be just the day that Emery left South Carolina. Shit, if not for the attack, maybe those dudes would have forgotten the date. I don't remember any significant move dates in my life. It would have just been another day.

*****

"It was a big deal, we were leaving." Matt told me. "All the parents were there. I tried to tell my parents

bye and started crying." Matt laughed at the memory of this. It's been well established that Matt lacks normal human emotions, like Mr. Spock. Logic and problem solving are the priority. But even Spock loved his mom. It's hard to leave your family to go far away, especially in an era where the only common tools for communication were just a plain ole' landline, and maybe an email from time to time. if you could "get to a computer."

I asked Devin how his parents felt about the move. "They didn't really love it." Everyone was sad. It's hard leaving home. Going off to college is one thing, but moving three thousand miles away is a different level of child-parent separation.

Toby's parents didn't quite react the same way. We will dive much deeper into Toby and his parents eventually, but for now, it's noteworthy to inform you that Toby was the only one of the group whose parents did not come to see him off. Matt described the scene of their departure: Toby was awkwardly standing off to the side while everyone else embraced their parents in tears. The loving parents were giving an emotional farewell to their babies. Toby's dad, on the other hand had this to say, and I quote, "Don't call me when you run out of money."

Out of context, I can see how this implies that his dad doesn't care about him. I don't think it was that at all. From everything I can tell about what I know about Toby's relationship with his parents, love is not absent. The best way to describe Mr. Morrell's attitude would be to call it tough love, I guess. Either way, he had no intention of shedding tears in public over his dumb ass son moving across the country to start a band.

After learning about the attacks on New York from the Cracker Barrel lady, the guys pondered the idea of going home. "Should we just go back and kind of wait it out?" Devin remembered thinking. It felt scary. But they obviously decided that it didn't really change anything, so they kept on going. Their parents wanted them to turn back, but then that would have meant the terrorists won.

A day or two later they passed through Chicago, and so they went downtown to check it out. The city was basically shut down. "It was like a ghost town man," Chopper told me. This trip was resoundingly boring, according to the guys; consisting of nothing but flat tires and camping. Aside from the first day with planes blowing up a couple buildings, nothing at all happened on this trip. After I interviewed everyone, I was so happy that I hadn't thought of writing a road trip book about the move to Seattle. They took three vehicles on the move, so it's not like when you picture a band in a van, trekking across the country, listening to music, and engaging in deep conversations.

The guys knew nothing about Seattle. They had nowhere to live. They had no jobs. They were just going to show up. In a way, they were like "settlers". It's not that crazy, really. Back in the ole days, you hear about a place where there is "opportunity" and you hitch up the wagon and show up. Remember the movie "Tombstone" where Wyatt Earp just rolls into town and slaps Billy Bob Thornton in the face, takes over a saloon, and finds a few lots to rent before he shoots the shit with Doc Holliday? That was Emery. Except with much less authority and bad assness.

"What kind of research did you do?" I asked Matt.

"Zero."

Like I said, they knew nothing about what they were getting into.

"We were terrified of cities and driving. I started getting nervous when we started getting fifty, forty, thirty [miles away]. I thought, 'Guys we need to get ready to pull off.' What if we get downtown and we have this trailer? We can't do downtown." The only place in the south that could possibly resemble driving in a big city would be Atlanta. But even then, it's just a lot of sitting in traffic on the interstate. The downtown driving isn't anything like New York, Philly, Chicago, San Francisco, or even Seattle. In Seattle, the city is right on top of the water. You just run out of room. The distance from Interstate 5 to the water can't be more than a mile. There are one-ways and crazy intersections with curvy roads running into straight roads that are really big hills. I love driving in big cities, but I would argue that downtown Seattle can be quite difficult to get comfortable in.

"I was afraid we could get stuck, or what if the police get us?" I love that. The police "getting them", like they were illegal immigrants or something. "GET THOSE FUCKING REDNECKS! THEY DON'T BELONG ROUND THESE PARTS!!"

The next part of the story is by far the best demonstration of Emery's small town roots. All they knew was that the Space Needle would be there somewhere. But, besides that they didn't really know what Seattle looked like.

"We got in and saw the skyline, 'We have to pull off now!' And we we're looking around like 'Where's the space needle? We pulled off and we saw a Safeway." They pulled into the parking lot to regroup and figure out what to do next. So now we have a bunch of might-as-well-be-foreigners standing around in a parking lot, looking around just in absolute awe. Matt continued, "We thought, 'This is awesome! This is big! But we can't find the space needle. I swear I know from pictures we should be able to see the space needle.'" One wouldn't think it would be so difficult to find a national landmark that sticks out like a sore thumb, even in the congested Seattle skyline. So where *was* the space needle?

"We were in Bellevue. We weren't even across Lake Washington yet. We were just at a Safeway in Bellevue, thought we were in Seattle, which is twelve miles across Lake Washington." Amazing. Once the guys realized they weren't in Seattle proper, they asked some people at the Safeway if there were any RV parks nearby. Somebody pointed them in the direction of Dash Point, a state park located about halfway between Seattle and Tacoma. They made their way down there and set up shop. Matt's exact words were that they thought, "Ok…this is safe." They would detach the trailer and go into the city to look for jobs and places to live. Oh wait…the trailer. I must tell you about the trailer.

Matt's dad had acquired a trailer from a guy in Greer that he used to transport go karts. It was big enough – twenty-four feet long to be exact - that the guys were able to build bunks and hook up a generator so they could have some power. There was even a piss bucket. Maybe more sophisticated than that, but for sure it was just something you would dump out the bottom of the trailer. Chopper, of course, had insight into the piss bucket situation. "We would pee in that toilet and it would just drain out wherever we were. We were in Portland staying outside some friend's house. They came outside to wave us off and we were driving down the road and we looked at them. They took a few steps forward and they were standing in our pee…puddle. Just this giant, piss spot right in the middle of the street."

The bunks were laid out such that you would have to crawl through one set of beds to get to the other set. So if you were going to sleep first, it was necessary to climb into one of the bunks closest to the back of the trailer, otherwise somebody would have to crawl over you. They brought this thing specifically so they would have somewhere to sleep when they arrived in Seattle.

It sounds like a dream to me. Not a literal dream, but a dream, as in, I love the idea. They loved it too. They lived at the park for several weeks until they were able to get settled into an apartment. Chopper referred to the lifestyle as "tribal." Just dudes working together to pursue a goal. It stresses me out to think about how far away they were from achieving those goals at this point in the process. But with a fantastic climate, beautiful scenery, and a grill, it doesn't take much to satisfy a group of men. I envy this experience and you should too. It makes me happy that all the members of the band look back on it in a fond manner.

*****

Matt and Joel got jobs at Guitar Center; land of the most obnoxious people on the face of the earth. I can't believe they let people just come in there and bang on the fucking drums. I always see the guys that work in the drum department on the phone, struggling to do their jobs because of the noise. It's even worse as a customer. "YEAH, I NEED TWO PAIRS OF PRO MARK 5B HICKORY. NO 5B. HICKORY! PRO MARK. NO NOT VIC FIRTH. PRO MARK. NO NOT PLASTIC TIPS, GODDAMMIT. WOOD TIP." Then you have to deal with buying everything from four different sales guys because they got to get their fucking commissions. So if your guitar player asks you to pick up some strings while you are picking up your sticks, it's a whole ordeal. Then they have to ask for your address and phone number and email. Why the hell do you need my address to buy drumsticks? It's insane. But, it's a really good job for musicians trying to tide themselves over until they can quit and go on tour. Good deals on gear. The problem is that most of those guys never get to quit and go on tour. Their pony tails just keep getting longer and longer. Then, the soul patch creeps in. Before you know it you are playing "gigs" and being named sales manager. Your fate is sealed. If you're lucky you will get your own store one day. And you will never, ever, play music for a living.

This is where the 'hipster' in the subtitle of this book comes into play. Josh Head was an employee of this particular Guitar Center. Being the great first impression guy that he is, Matt and Chopper became friends with Josh, and eventually he started hanging around with the other guys in the band. Devin remembered Matt and Joel inviting Josh over after they moved out of their racing trailer and into an apartment. "They brought him over, and you know everybody loves Josh at first glance. When you first meet him, it's more like the fun guy, and there's something cool about him. Obviously, there's other things that come up later but…" Devin ended this statement with an endearing laugh. But Emery started to learn about Josh and his "quirks" fairly quickly. "Josh…I think he would admit this to a certain degree; he's real just kind of hit or miss with, like, his attention and his focus on stuff, " Devin said. Josh had been in school for recording and had a makeshift studio set up at his house. Josh told the guys that he would record them for free. So they scheduled a night to come work on some demos.

Devin went on, "We had known him for a few months, or whatever. But we found out he had a home studio." By the way, every band that has ever started in any city anywhere has known the guy with a home studio that could record demos for them. Not once in the history of the world has one of those demos ever sounded good. "We were going to record a demo with him one night," says Devin "and we show up at his house and he's not there. So I think Matt called him or something and he was like, 'Oh yeah, yeah,' kind of his Josh thing, 'ummm.'"

On a totally different night, they had a similar experience trying to get some demos recorded. "One night we got there and he was with his girlfriend, and, you know, they were probably doing stuff in the bedroom." Devin told me they just kind of waited outside for awhile until Josh finally got done with his appointment. "Eventually he came and let us in and we started working and we were like, 'Matt! Who's this guy? What are you doing here?' So eventually we got it done, but it was real flaky."

"So what prompted, 'Hey, lets let the flaky guy in the band?'" I asked Devin.

"It was more like...you know, all the positive aspects of his personality. So, once he became close with us, he went to all the shows with us, and he would kind of help us, or whatever."

"I became the buddy who went to the show and sold t-shirts." Josh said. So there is always the guy that can make your demos, but then there is always the guy that will just hang around and sell your t-shirts, too. Josh just happened to be both. Actually, it turns out that Josh is pretty smart because he just eventually danced himself right into the band. I love the way Devin explained it.

"Matt kind of played some keyboards and guitar, and eventually he was like, 'You know, I could just show Josh these couple parts, and he could come up here and play on certain parts and kind of step off,' or whatever. And then the first time that [Josh] did that…when he wasn't playing, he just started dancing," Devin said with growing laughter. "We were like 'I guess that's awesome? I guess we will keep him in there.'"

So that was Emery. Toby, Matt, Devin, Chopper, Seth, and now Josh. What a fucking terrible business model. Six people? Goodness.

*****

The guys were getting ready to move out of their apartment and into a house with a basement. Rent ain't cheap in Seattle, but with everyone pitching in, it was worth it to try and have a "band house" for them to be able to practice and demo in with everyone living there. Josh was just kind of couch surfing at the apartment because it was close to the Guitar Center they worked at, but he was going to move into the new house with the whole band. It all sounded like a pretty good plan.

One day while prepping to move, Matt and Toby were sweeping out the trailer. They were about to drop $3K on a deposit for this new house. Lightning struck their brains– I believe the recounting of the conversation somewhat differs on details depending on who you talk to – but one of them basically said, "Hey let's NOT move into this house, save the money and just go on tour. Live in this trailer." And then the other guy said, "Yes. Let's do it."

Josh was at work when this all went down. "I came home from work one day and they were like 'Instead of spending three-thousand dollars to put down to rent this house right now, let's just go on tour.' I was like 'Ok?'" Josh called his parents in nearby Maple Valley and asked if they could crash at their house. Half the band would sleep inside and the other half would sleep in the race car trailer. There was a property with two garages right next to Josh's parents' house, so the band rented it for cheap and set up a practice room and studio to demo. They soundproofed it to not bother the neighbors, and even ran cables to different rooms for recording purposes.

"Who wouldn't want to do that? It sounds extreme, but what would be more fun than that?
We'll just drive to California and get gigs, and if we get one in Arizona, we will go there." Matt couldn't fathom that anyone would be against this whole idea of not getting the house and living free. There was at least one, though. Chopper hated this idea at first. "I was adamantly against [not getting in the house]. It's good it worked out." I think to make it as a band, you have to make drastic and uncomfortable decisions for the greater good of the band. Cutting down living expenses and other financial responsibilities is a key factor. You've GOT to be able to get up and go. "That's the thing. The more bills you have, you might not be able to play a last-minute show because you might have to work or something." That's right, Chopper. You get it.

In addition to the scaling back and the DIY recording set up, they created a basically communistic economic system. Matt was the leader of the Emery

Communist Party. "Everything was communal. We didn't have our own money at that time. We did all shared money from that point. One tube of toothpaste. We'd spend eight dollars at the grocery store and that was everybody's food." This is my least favorite part of trying to make it as a band. I could never go back to it. I like to be in charge of what I eat. I'm a libertarian. I don't even always eat the same thing as my wife for dinner. I have food anxiety. There ain't no way I could ever let Toby go pick out what I was going to eat at the grocery store. That's exactly who they would send, too, because Toby was a cheap ass motherfucker.

Matt continued. "I designed a system where I say, 'Here's what we're gonna do. Everyone can go work, get your job, whatever you want to do. Seventy-five percent of the money you make will be community. Twenty-five percent you can do whatever you want to.' Of course that's a good idea." Young band dudes are pretty irresponsible, and there is always the guy that doesn't have enough to cover his share of rent, or pitch in for gas, or whatever. I've been there. I've been that guy myself. But, I say it's a fantastic idea to centralize everything. If four dudes are bad with their money, but one guy is really good at managing a mutual fund, why not? You are all moving towards the same goal. Relieve some pressure from each individual member and make one big pot. I love communism in very small doses, and six dudes living together in a trailer is a pretty small dose. But it must be voluntary. In the case of Emery, they decided communism was the best thing for them at that time.

Chopper warmed up to the idea as it went along. "You can't live like that very long. There's a time where you can have no responsibilities and have your band make it. You can only be homeless for so long. But, I had less to worry about." Because they were set up this way, they could just hit the road whenever they felt like it. They were only paying Josh's parents $700/month, which was easy to cover out of the communal pot of money. Emery had the freedom to drive down to California and hang around Huntington Beach for a week. Play shows. Do nothing. Whatever. Basically they had their home base in the trailer. So they were essentially just moving to places for short periods of time and trying to get shows, or meet people. It was loose. It's a great way to live your life, at least for awhile.

This was all fun for them, but none of it mattered if

they weren't making progress towards their goal of getting a record deal. They were already playing a lot of the songs that ended up being on "The Weak's End," but they were super rough around the edges. "We knew what we had to do was make a real record," was Matt's mindset. A "real record" meant finding a known producer to take on their band, likely unsigned. That was likely to be an uphill battle if they wanted to record with someone that "mattered." But Emery had been defying what should be possible ever since they set off on 9/11. The band was still together in Seattle almost two years later. Nobody had bailed back to South Carolina, except for Seth's short stint going off the relationship deep end – but they were really doing it. Their commitment had been established. All their efforts put them on the verge of a completely written album, and in search of a place to record the album that would launch them into the screamo scene for good.

9

A NIGHT WITH
"THE SHAMAN"

There is an episode of "Seinfeld" where

Kramer's first name is finally revealed to be "Cosmo". At
first, Kramer is embarrassed by his friends finding out
after having successfully hid it from them for so many
years, simply being known to the world as "Kramer". By
the end of the episode, Kramer has embraced his given
name and wants the world to know. Cosmo struts down
the streets of New York City greeting everyone, receiving
shout outs from across the street and apartment windows.
He is the man of the neighborhood. Everyone knows

Cosmo Kramer. Everyone loves Cosmo Kramer. Cosmo Kramer is the fucking man. In this sense, Josh Head is Cosmo Kramer and Cosmo Kramer is Josh Head.

The Shaman - Josh's nickname whose origin is unknown to me - rules his neighborhood with mystery and charm. The Capital Hill neighborhood in Seattle is the hippest, grungiest, crustiest, anything goes neighborhood in the Northwest. Walking through Capitol Hill with Josh Head is like walking through the Upper West Side with Cosmo Kramer. Josh is waving to people, getting stopped on the street to chat, locals literally shouting from across the street to greet him. He's been there so damn long that he has become a staple to the neighborhood. He is tall and very good looking. Everyone says he has that kind of Jim Caviezel as Jesus Christ thing going on, but more hipster. He's as mysterious, though. Like how did Jesus make money or live? The same question could be asked about Josh. How the hell does he survive in Seattle? Emery is nowhere close to a full time band anymore. Actually Jesus, Kramer, and Josh are all similar in a lot of ways. They just kind of "walk the earth" and get by somehow. We don't know a whole lot about any of them. All great first impression types. All full of crazy ideas.

While Josh and I sat at the bar of this stupidly expensive Japanese restaurant in Capitol Hill, I asked him, "What's the game plan, man? What do you want to do in life?"

He told me he wanted to start a record label, a podcast and basically help creatives get their art − whatever medium it may be − out to the people. I have the exact quotes about this later on in this chapter but it's funny and interesting because that is exactly what his long-time bandmates, Matt and Toby, have spent the last 3 years building. The plan was that he would launch a kickstarter for his solo record, and then parlay that into building his label from there. That kickstarter was supposed to happen in January of 2016. It has not happened at the time of this book being published. There is no label. There is no creative think tank. There is nothing. Josh runs sound at a pretty cool local venue and flies out to play Emery shows a few times a year. Maybe he does some other stuff that nobody is aware of. Again, who the hell knows how Kramer pays rent on the Upper East Side of Manhattan across the hall from a successful comedian.

I need to be careful in the way I address this. I have tried to be honest throughout this entire book about my assessment of the members of Emery and the band's career. Part of the reason it's difficult to write about Josh and his role in Emery is because there has been so much swept under the rug in this band as it pertains to Josh and his relationship to the rest of the band. It is true that he is an outsider in many ways. He's from Seattle and he didn't grow up with the other guys. He's the new guy. There are some things that are naturally going to be lost in translation between a bunch of rednecks and a Northwestern hipster. Josh exists in a totally different vibe of life than Matt, Toby, Devin, Dave, Chopper, Seth or anyone else that has ever played in this band.

Josh stays up all night. He sleeps late into the day. Josh disappears for hours exploring a city looking for good coffee. Josh hasn't married and miraculously has not impregnated a woman yet. I'm only speculating, but Josh is likely quite the ladies man. Like I said, he is extremely good looking. I mean, I'd fuck him if I was a chick. Shit, I'd fuck him if I was a dude. I am a dude…but I have not fucked him…yet.

Josh has the luxury of living this adult man-child

type of lifestyle. I promise I don't mean that as a criticism. Responsibility is overrated, and for people that live in big cities and are ok with a sort of bohemian type of life, I would say it is likely a very satisfying life. Josh can do what he wants, when he wants. Nobody else in Emery can say that. That is a freedom that every married man – as happy as they may be – longs for.

There may even be jealousy between the rest of the band and Josh. From the perspective of the other guys, his life is just easier. As the keyboard player and dancer-in-chief, his role in the daily operations of the band - whether it's logistical or creative - are in all actuality quite minimal. Josh isn't a song writer. He isn't a business guy. He's kind of just there, like a trophy wife. But the harsh truth is nobody would give a shit about Emery shows without Josh. Fans fucking love him.

What follows is the majority of my 3-hours' worth of conversation with Josh as we bar hopped around Capitol Hill on a cold and rainy night. To give a true sense of Emery's hippest and most beautiful member, I have made the decision that the best way is to let him tell you. The rest of this chapter is going to be laid out similar to that of a magazine article to maximize Josh's voice over my own. Ladies and gents, I give you, The Shaman.

*****

A: Well, I'm here…

J: How was your flight?

A: Well, I woke up at four AM my time but I got here at eleven. I went to Storyville in the market. Hung out there. Met up with Chris [Lott].

J: Yeah, Storyville. That's some crappy coffee shop.

A: Is it?

J: (Laughs) It's so fancy.

A: You have a couch or something?

J: No…my bed.

A: I was gonna go stay with Matt, but I thought if I'm

already here...

J: Yeah, you could, uh...if my roommate is not coming home then there's a whole another bedroom.

A: Yeah, find out if they're coming home. Matt already said I could stay with them. I just gotta wait on them to get home.

J: They live way up north.

A: How far?

J: I don't know, actually. Probably a 20-minute drive without traffic.

A: Welp, writing a book on Emery.

J: Yeah...what's it going to be about?

A: Emery.

The bartender brought us our chips and salsa. We

were sitting at the bar of a fancy Mexican joint. The type of Mexican joint where you pay six dollars for chips and salsa and three dollars a pop for street tacos. It's the worst kind of Mexican restaurant. But damn the chips and salsa were pretty good.

J: They make the tortillas here.

A: I know. I saw that on the window.

My phone actually stopped recording right here and I have no idea exactly for how long. But we were talking about me crashing with Josh, which prompted me to begin questioning him about his living situation. I knew that at one point he owned a condo, but I didn't know all the details about what happened. I had suspected it had something to do with the housing market crash, which actually has affected several members of Emery. The recording of our conversation picked up with us discussing Josh losing his condo.

J: So, one month I just didn't get a check, a paycheck from the band. So, I called Ed (Emery's business manager at the time) and was like, "Hey I didn't get a check or direct deposit," and he's like, "Oh there's no money in the band account." I'm like, oh! I wish somebody at any point during this month would have told me so that if I wasn't expecting to get paid I could've worked 'cause I need to pay my mortgage. So I paid my mortgage on my credit cards for six months. Maxed out.

A: I didn't know you could do that.

J: Apparently you can. Well it's illegal now, but Wells Fargo did it just to screw people over, and they got sued by [the state of] Washington, and I got some of the money back. I got screwed out of 30 or 40 thousand dollars in that whole situation after like 3 years of trying to make my mortgage work. Then the state of Washington sued Wells Fargo class action, and I got back fifteen hundred bucks. Alright cool, I guess I'll pay my rent for a few months.

A: How long were you able to stay in the house?

J: Oh, well, foreclosure is a long process. It took about six months. Me and my brother bought it together and after about six or seven months in, we decided to rent it out. And so we did the craigslist thing, and rented it out to this lady. So, two or three months in, she stopped paying us. And then the eviction process also takes six months. So, she was in there for six months not paying us at all. I was going to use that to try and refinance, but eventually we just had to fully foreclose.

A: You were going to be like, "Hey, this is an income property now"?

J: Yeah, so [we] fully foreclosed. Bank took it back. Bank sold it, then the bank sued my brother and me for like sixty grand, which we had lost 'cause we had owed them around two hundred grand on that condo. So then I had to file for bankruptcy. They froze my bank account. So I talked to a lawyer, and the lawyer was like, "Well sometimes your income isn't high enough that they won't come after you." They can look at your bank account. Get a court order. I couldn't use a debit. I had like no money.

A: You had nothing? And no way to get it, either?

J: Yeah, I had to start cashing my paychecks at like a check cashing place just to pay my rent because I couldn't open a bank account. I couldn't open another bank account because the other bank would see it and go, "You have a frozen bank account? Why?" It's a fucking long story. Shitty ass world.

A: All because Emery didn't write "The Question" part two.

J: Yeah, all because of "I'm Only a Man". Thanks a lot, Toby.

A: I remember, though, after that came out, me and you were sitting on the bus talking about it. And I mean, you were stoked on it.

J: Oh yeah. I loved that record.

A: And you said you felt like you guys made a timeless record.

J: I did.

A: But commercially…

J: This is gonna sound stupid…it's our "Sam's Town" from The Killers. Their weirdest record, but my favorite of theirs. That little odd ball of a record. Listening to it now, it's not as congruent song to song. It's a little eclectic as far as style throughout the record.

Don't misunderstand Josh. He isn't actually comparing Emery to The Killers. The Killers are in my opinion one of the greatest bands of our generation. Emery has fans that believe they are the greatest band of their generation, but that's because fans are insane. Josh used The Killers as an example here because Josh has impeccable taste in music. He really does. Honestly Josh would probably be better suited as a DJ than a keyboardist/screamer in a band like Emery. The point is that The Killers did what they wanted to do on "Sam's Town". Emery did the same on "I'm Only a Man". The difference is that The Killers still had some hits. "I'm Only a Man" fell flat.

A: So do you think if y'all just made "The Question" part two…[you] would have sold half a million records?

J: You mean if we had made "In Shallow Seas"?

A: Yeah.

J: No. I mean it would have done better than "I'm Only a Man," but I think the way we know now how the music industry was doing…It still sold thirteen thousand copies the first week.

A: Oh it did?

J: But everyone was thinking thirty.

A: How much did "The Question" sell first week?

J: Twenty [thousand]. People were thinking it would be much bigger, which makes sense, but "The Weak's End" sold two, or fifteen hundred, or something first week.

A: As Cities Burn first week did four.

J: Yeah, we broke the record with our debut, and then you guys.

A: Yeah, that was a big deal

J: Haste the Day broke it, and then you guys still have the record.

A: The Chariot had the biggest, but I say that doesn't count because of Scogin.

J: Yeah, that doesn't. Sorry Josh, don't count.

Josh kept leaning into the mic on my phone to emphasize statements.

A: Just to be clear, nobody is ever gonna hear this. This isn't for entertainment value, just for me.

J: Oh yeah, ok. Fuck you, Josh Scogin. Fuck everyone. Fuck you all.

A: I can quote you. We are on the record.

J: This is on the record. Fuck everyone. Fuck the New England Patriots.

I didn't really know anything about how Josh grew up. There was always some mystery behind why Josh is the way he is. I have a pre-conceived notion of Pacific Northwest folks being weirdo hippies. Josh's recounting his experience growing up in a small town of hippies only served to reinforce my notions.

J: The town I was from is four hundred people, out by Mt. Rainier. It was started in the late 1890's? It was a coal mining town, and back then there was [sic] five thousand people. It was a big industry there, and there were trains running out there. The town is named after the guy that owned the town, Wilkinson, but the guy never actually set foot in the town, ever. So it's kind of a crazy spot. It's kind of not really hippie, but people that don't wanna be bothered. There's not a stop sign or stop light. My parents are hippies, and my dad wanted to

throw a party for his hippie friends. Must have been in
like 1977?

A: Awesome drugs?

J: Yeah. Awesome drugs.

A: Orgies?

J: I don't know about orgies. Dad, were you into orgies?
I don't know. I don't think so.

Josh's parents ended up in this town on a whim.
They became caretakers of a property owned by a retired
European couple. It was eighty-five acres and on sale for
$250,000 in the late seventies. Nobody ever bought it.
Josh's parents moved into a shed with no plumbing or
electricity, but it was free. Joe Head, Josh's dad, picked
up a hitchhiker that became his best friend, Mike. Turns
out it was their closest neighbor that lived a mile away.
Mike and his wife Marge had a kid, Mike Jr. One day,
Mike Jr. walked up to Joe Head and asked, "Hey, Joe. Do
you know who Jesus is?"

"No, not really" Joe Head replied. And that's the night Josh's dad became a Christian. Because a five-year-old Mike Jr. had learned about Jesus in Sunday school that day. Josh's parents got married out on the property, and his dad's buddies built log cabins for everyone to live in. 'Everyone' consisted of Mike and Marge and a few other families. These log cabins did have plumbing and running water, but still no electricity.

J: I didn't have electricity until we moved when I was fourteen; never had it. There was a payphone in town about a mile and half away that I would ride my bike to and call my friends at the post office.

A: What friends?

J: Church! There was [sic] only four hundred people in town.

Basically, Josh is implying that having friends in a town with only four hundred weirdos living there isn't that hard. Although I'm not sure why they had phones and Josh didn't.

A: Homeschool?

J: Mmhmm. I homeschooled 'til college.

A: Wow. So you never played sports or anything?

J: I played little league. I played baseball in that town.

A: But no school organized--

J: No. I played baseball. I played rugby when I was in high school [in a league] for non-school sanctioned kids.

A: Were you the oldest?

J: Yeah, I'm the oldest; two younger brothers.

A: So how'd you get into music?

J: In high school when I was seventeen, my parents moved into Maple Valley, which is where Seth lives now. This is the house where everyone in the band lived for awhile - when we decided we wanted to make it. I had two best friends, one played bass, one played guitar. And they were like, "You need to learn how to play drums and lets start a band." I never played a single instrument, and I was seventeen years old.

A: I mean…what did you know about music? You didn't even have electricity.

J: Nothing. Nothing. I listened to music a little bit, in the car.

It wasn't until around the time that his parents moved back into civilization that Josh really got into music. Seattle in these days was a great place to do so, luckily for Josh. He got turned on to Nirvana, Rage Against the Machine, and Helmet. For a kid growing up without access to things like, oh, electricity, I'm surprised Josh was able to find quality music so quickly after moving out of butt fucked Egypt.

J: The homeschooling was half hippie, half Jesus movement type stuff where they just thought the public school system was bad. We lived so far outside of town that the school bus didn't run there. It wasn't a weird thing. Half of my friends went to [public school] and half of my friends homeschooled.

When his new and normal friends asked him to learn to play drums, he was totally lost. How does a kid that grew up pissing in an outhouse and living by candlelight have any idea about music education? I'm assuming his homeschool network didn't have a marching band option.

J: When I started playing drums I didn't know what 4/4 meant. I didn't know what downbeat meant. Now they will tell you the first couple times we would play together they didn't think that I could do it. Finally, it clicked with me. One day, I listened to a song on the radio and I was like, "Oh I get it. This is like repeating."

A: It's a beat!

Josh is tapping on the table, excitedly detailing his realization of what makes a song. His tapping is exquisite. There is a way that drummers and those with rhythm tap with their hands. It's a feel. Josh has the feel.

A: Did y'all have a name?

J: Aww Shucks.

A: Aww Shucks was your band name? Oh man.

We ordered a second round of drinks; the next round of many future rounds on this night.

J: I was in a band at college with my roommates. They kicked me out.

A: Why did they kick you out?

J: I just...I was really bad at time management back then. Working a lot, and school, and I dropped out, and they didn't think I was committed enough to be in the band.

A: Were they trying to like, "make it?" They wanted to like...take it somewhere?

J: I guess kind of, yeah. So I was like, ok. That's fine. I was in my first serious relationship then; my first girlfriend, Elaine, who all the guys in the band know; Lanie.

A: Elaine?

J: Yeah. "Seinfeld."

A: I've never known an Elaine.

I sound like a total creep on the tape here. Like the weirdo TV Guide guy from that episode of Seinfeld. Look, I'm never going to stop making Seinfeld references in my books. Just deal with it and watch the show so we can be on the same page.

J: She goes by Lanie. She changed her name.

A: Did she change her name because of "Seinfeld?"

Jerry called Elaine "Lanie" sometimes, so, it

wouldn't have done any good.

J: No, I don't think so. I think she liked the name.

A: So you got kicked out of that band. Anything after that?

J: Emery.

*****

I debated in my head whether or not to spend money on the expensive Mexican food. Some of the menu items sounded really good, but I couldn't pull the trigger. I was full from a ramen lunch where I ordered extra noodles because I think my life is a fucking travel show. I'm sure it would have been amazing. Actually, why am I sure of that? Now that I think of it, maybe the tortillas weren't as good as I remember.

Josh and I spent quite awhile discussing how he joined the band and what the early days before they were signed were like. It's well-established that he was the last to come along outside of the original crew from South

Carolina. But what's funny to me is that the guy from the big city of Seattle - home of Nirvana – wouldn't end up influencing Emery's music in some earthshattering way. He didn't even play keyboards when he was asked to join the band. He didn't play anything on "The Weak's End" other than a few overdubs.

J: I didn't do anything; just sat there for ten days.

So what WAS Josh doing in Emery? If you ask any Emery fan about an Emery live show, they will immediately start telling you about the crazy keyboard player that walks on the heads of the crowd and dances like Michael Jackson to screamo jams. We were discussing the trend of bands going absolutely ape shit during our early years coming up in the hardcore/emo scene.

J: I think Refused probably had a lot to do with that for a lot of bands. For me, it was Zach De La Rocha from Rage [Against the Machine]. You could see videos of them on MTV, and I had their live VHS.

A: Limp Bizkit. Wes Boreland did some pretty crazy stuff, I guess.

Listening back to me bringing up Limp Bizkit is embarrassing. Why the fuck did I interject Limp Bizkit into this conversation about Refused and Rage? Now Limp Bizkit is in this book.

A: To me, Zach was the most intense person on stage ever. You see videos of him just like, shaking, and just going crazy. I used to do this move where I used to put my fists behind my back, like way up high. That's Zach de Larocha all the way. I stole that move from him. He just had the microphone and one hand behind his back and he'd just be so mad.

Josh is passionate about this topic. This is his wheelhouse – putting on the show and positioning himself as the main event, if you will.

J: Once I got comfortable - I'm not super comfortable socially, but stage is different. I'm not super comfortable unless I'm in a group of people. But on stage, it's like,

"Yeah, I can try this Usher dance move I saw that's funny." Then it was like, this is music and dancing that I like and enjoy, so I just decided one day - why can't stuff that boy bands do or pop artists…why can't stuff that Michael Jackson does look cool for a hardcore band? So I just started doing stuff like that.

Somehow it works. Fans like it. It *is* different. Nobody else in the scene really moves the way Josh does on stage. Everyone throws guitars around their necks and tomahawks their headstocks into the singers face.

J: I thought it's at least a weird contrast. And it's fun. And I'm also not wasting as much energy or oxygen now. I don't have to thrash around. I can just be a little bit coy and playful and kind of give a middle finger to the aggression of our scene. Back then, our lyrics were all about heartbreak, but the show looked like you're trying to fight somebody. All the mosh pits are like fighting, but the song's about some girl breaking your heart. That's *all* the bands. I thought that was really funny. I was like, "I don't need to throw my fist around anymore 'cause I'm not angry about anything. I'm actually having a really good time."

My view of Josh's role in the band has been uncomfortable for me in the past; definitely more so when I was as their tour manager. If I'm being honest, I have often wondered why Josh was still in the band. Why would he WANT to still be in the band? His musical role is minimal. Yet I think there is some validity to the idea that he is really important to the live shows, and fans expect to see him there over in his corner dancing the night away.

If you spend any significant time with Emery on the road, or have a candid conversation with different members, it's easy to see the disconnect between Josh and the rest of the band. But I'm serious when I say that this band all gets along REALLY well. There is nothing about Josh's relationship with the band that inhibits anything with regards to atmosphere, morale, or functionality. I mean, Matt and Toby argue constantly. Josh is really kind of chill as fuck.

But still, there's the disconnect. What is it? Whatever it is, it started a long time ago. Josh's recounting of Emery finally signing their record deal with

Tooth and Nail was a bit awkward to listen to.

J: I didn't sign. I had been in the band for almost a year. Matt grabs me and said, "Hey man, just so you know, everyone else is going to sign, but you're not going to. It's going to be like original members signing." And I was like…okay. So, yeah, whatever. I ended up officially being in the band for "The Question," a couple years later.

A: What was the reason for that you think?

J: I…I…I don't know…It was probably because I didn't write anything on the record anyway. I just recorded some overdubs for keyboard parts. I'm not really sure; the signing thing.

Josh paused, possibly suppressing some genuine hurt feelings that maybe he wasn't comfortable communicating to me, which I would say is totally understandable. The story was borderline humiliating. Well, that's coming from someone who has a tremendous amount of pride. I would have quit the fucking band right then and there, perhaps for no good reason. Josh is a bit more level-headed in this regard, or at least he seems to be.

J: I remember being kind of bummed at the time, but only because they told me the day we were driving up there to sign. I was still in the office while everyone was signing and was just skipped over with the paperwork. It would have been cool to tell me maybe the day before, or something.

A: That is a very Emery thing I would say.

J: Yeah.

A: Well, it's a very Matt and Toby thing.

J: Yeah.

A: I could see the argument I guess?

The argument to be made is that Josh didn't write or play on the record, and therefore should not be entitled to any sort of royalties paid out because of the success of the record. I definitely get it. But I do agree with Josh on taking issue with the timing.

J: Well, yeah…I mean, it didn't bother me. It was just the timing. It was awkward for me. I wasn't even upset or mad. When I finally did sign, I was sitting in the studio half way through "The Question" and Jon Dunn dropped by with the paperwork. There was no celebration. I had been touring with the band for 2 years at that point.

Josh didn't really play or write much of anything for "The Question" either.

A: What should we do? I definitely have more I want to talk to you about. Should we mosey on?

Josh suggested that we make our way over to a chic Japanese joint where his friend Nick is the head bartender. Josh said something about how Nick wins awards – World's best bartender. I don't know. It's some bullshit from a yuppie magazine like Food and Wine. I'm a subscriber by the way.

The rain kicked our ass on the way over to Nick's bar. When we arrive, I removed all of my layers except my hoodie because I don't wear t-shirts under hoodies. Even though it's cold and miserably wet outside, when I listen back to the recording, there is a comfort in the air. This feeling that we are in a hip neighborhood, it's late at night, and you can dip into a nice bar and receive much needed hospitality. The word from Josh was that we were about to get a major hookup. We just needed to wait on Nick to arrive.

A: Bunda said something very interesting to me the other night.

J: Yeah?

A: NICK Bunda.

Nick Bunda is an Emery tour manager and he does a lot of work for BadChristian. He's most certainly an integral part of this world I am exploring. But his statements I am about to quote are grandiose, to say the least.

J: Yeah, go ahead, but he doesn't know anything about the world...

Bunda is only twenty-six years old. Little baby in the eyes of the old as fuck Emery dudes.

A: He said that, "Josh Head is the single most important member of Emery."

J: Interesting. I might disagree.

A: Yeah, I told him, "I might disagree with you there."

J: Yeah. Toby.

A: Yeah, I would guess Toby. He said that if Josh Head left the band and people came to the show, people would say, "Where's the guy that dances crazy and puts on the crazy show?" And they're gonna stop coming to the shows.

J: Yeah. *Maybe*. There might be some people that would do that, but it would be worse for the band if Toby left and Matt or I took over singing.

(Bartender interrupts)

A: Sorry, we didn't look.

J: Yeah…just stall.

Until the hookup master Nick arrives that is.

A: Mmmmmmm. Sochu.

J: There's so many aspects of a band. You got the writing and recording process that wouldn't happen without Matt. And then you have the songs that wouldn't happen without Toby.

The next ten minutes were spent discussing Toby and the torture that is arguing with Toby and how absurd Toby can be. But this is Josh's chapter. We will get to

Toby, I promise.

The bartender returned to check on us. We were taking up seats and not ordering. If we can just wait a few minutes, Nick will be here and shower us with free Old Fashions and sushi.

J: Maybe I'll start with a drink…

A: I'm going to start with a Tecate.

Bartender: You want lime?

A: Yeah, why not?!

We started discussing the menu. This place has a bar menu and a dining room menu. The bar menu is much smaller and less enticing than that of the dining room menu, but we stay put.

J: I don't know. We can wait until Nick gets here. He'll be here in like ten minutes.

There was more Toby talk, and then I expressed my

admiration for Emery staying together as long as it has. The degree of difficulty for everyone to keep it going to at least some degree is not lost on me or Josh.

A: There's this understanding. "Hey, we're doing this!"

J: Yeah, well when everyone except for me is married and has kids…

A: Let's talk about that real quick. I would guess that you would be open to putting more time into Emery?

J: Oh yeah. Yeah, for sure. When that started happening…it was Matt or Toby that called…

Emery was making not near the money they used to on recent tours. Recent, as in since about 2009. The scaling back was gradual. Toby started working at churches. Dave started working for his brother in law. Matt broke it down for Josh.

J: Matt was like, "I'm gonna start doing studio stuff. We're all gonna slow down and probably not tour as much. You're the only one who would tour more than we do for financial reasons." I could have been like, "Yeah ok. I'll just quit the band." I don't know. To me it doesn't seem weird to understand your friends station in life. That's where they're going. That's where my band is going. It's just gonna happen. No reason to get pissed off about it. I wish I toured more. I would.

A: Well as the single most important member of the band in Emery you would think...

I got a good chuckle out of Josh there.

J: We've definitely turned down tours recently where I wish we would have gone to do them more than other people. Like some European stuff just for traveling purposes. It wouldn't be as much money. I don't have mouths to feed. I don't have a wife that's going to miss me while I'm gone, either.

A: Single life is really easy.

J: Yeah, it's much easier. I mean, it's stressful too. I mean, still single at thirty-six is a little…

A: Is that important to you? To get married and have kids?

J: Yeah, to some degree. I mean I don't want to have a five-year old when I'm fifty. I don't want that. There's a little bit of uhh…some urgency; a little bit.

I could tell he was contemplating the consequences of "settling down"; taking stock of his life and being reminded of the advantages of his situation.

J: I get to live in a cool neighborhood. If I wanna take two weeks off work, I don't have as many bills. I can financially be stable much easier than somebody with a family.

A: Ok so…Emery's not full-time, or even close to full-time anymore. So what do you see for yourself moving towards?

J: Uh… right now? A lot. There's like a lot of…probably

more things than I can commit time to, which is a problem. I've always been really bad at time management anyway. Uh... so picking projects. So I'm...going...to put out...my own record.

Silence

A: Right on.

J: Yeah, so Kickstarter that. Starting in...January, I think. Uhhh...um. So I'm working on like the website. I've bought the domain names and the website. Working on all that right now. Uh... and then...I wanna put that out and then I actually want to...start my own...label to put it out. Which is a big undertaking because I wanna start a uh...I don't really know what it's going to be called...it's gonna be a label. Yeah. I wanna put out other artists, in all types of art forms besides music – painters, photographers, writers. Uhhhh...I wanna sign this street...this homeless street performer that performs three blocks away from here that I think is really, really amazing and bums for change and dollar bills. I don't know his story or why he's homeless, but his music is really good. Its just acoustic, he sings really well. Uhhh, yeah…I wanna do - at some point try to balance like doing a campaign for my record, doing a campaign for a label that's gonna look around to like help artists who don't know they can monetize their art, to monetize it. Even if it's like…even if I can make that guy $50 bucks a week that's like…you have an art form that is good. If your art's good, it does have value. Let me help you do that and I wanna set up the label. I think a label should function on more of a management principle as far as what money they take from an artist as opposed to the label side. I would set the label up to take like ten percent. It would be a flip of a record deal. Instead of the band getting fifteen points[2], the label would get fifteen. I think there's the ability that you can market and distribute digitally with a lot of things, and as a small company where you don't need…I don't need…even a 50/50 deal to me is too much money to give to a label. That's not much. 50/50 deal in the long run is like if you got twenty-five points from a record about. Maybe even twenty points. Because your profit depends on what the label is

---

[2] *Points on a record deal are similar to a percentage, but not really, but kind of. It's complicated, folks. Go read a book about it.

spending, so even though its a 50/50 deal on paper its not much better than fifteen points. It's not that great.

A: Right.

J: So I think there's a way to do that, not having crunched a lot of numbers. But I know from what our costs are. There's a friend here who I think is a great visual artist, and he makes these books that are amazing and these drawings, and he paints houses and office buildings and makes his money that way. He does art shows every once in a while and makes a few hundred dollars, and I'm like, "Man, there's people that do that stuff that like, if people outside of this local community knew about you, you could have a steady trickle of money coming in. Just a little bit."

A: Right.

J: So that's what I'm trying to do. So hopefully if I can get enough money from the campaign for my solo record just off Emery fans thinking it's cool, then I'll actually use that money to do this label.

A: So you want to stay involved in music?

J: Oh, I want to do music. I like music. I know a lot about it, you know. I like, understand how it works. I understand how, you know, the varying things that go into marketing and selling music. I know I understand all that; social media and internet marketing. All those things I've done. I have all the tools to do that. I don't really have the…you know, if I signed…if I got a street performer off the street or something electronic…

We got interrupted by a female friend of Josh's. This is more of the Kramer thing I was talking about.

J: Umm, yeah…so I think that I could like…I think there is opportunity for so much good art and music that gets lost. Bands that break up, or a guy who doesn't realize his stuff is good because he has to go get a job, so he stops making music because he doesn't have time because he can't afford it. But if someone who is a bartender, but also happens to be really good at making little electronic beats or plays in a cool little punk band, and if you could record it and do things for cheap enough and get something out there and keep the costs down and they could make…if they could just recoup the cost of doing a record then they might have been a band for longer. I just think of other bands that we played with back in the day that were so good that just stopped doing it because they were investing so much money of their own into this project that they never get any of it back. So, I think it would help contribute to, you know, art and the community as a whole. And hopefully that's good and I wouldn't want it to be, uh, have any type of Christian…I wanna put out all types of artists.

At this point we somehow digressed into a conversation about Satanists and how they are actually pretty nice people. I suggested they change their name. Satanist just sounds pretty harsh. Josh has Satanist friends, apparently. Eventually, we got back to Josh's plans for an artistic incubator empire.

J: I wanna…and then yeah, that's my idea. That's what I wanna do. It's a lot of time to do it. So I'm trying to reach out to a few friends in Seattle that might be interested in helping 'cause yeah, I don't have enough time to do it all on my own. I want people with varying ideologies and beliefs to be a part of the label. One reason that I want to also - I don't know if I would be a part of it, but uh - I would like to start and curate…umm…a podcast.

I was a little taken aback by the prospect of this. I have a hard time understanding why he wants to do exactly everything that his bandmates are doing. But in his mind, this creative pursuit would be way different than that of Matt and Toby's.

J: It would be three or four hosts, all of varying religious, political, sexual…like my friend group of people. No one in my friend group is Christian. So I would love to tackle just day to day bullshit conversation, and also current event issues, social issues, and show that like, here's three or four people that believe totally different things and they can argue about stuff, but they're friends. They get along and this is how, like, community is supposed to work in my mind.

Finally, Nick showed up and gave me some spiel

about the documentary "Jiro Dreams of Sushi" and the way that the kitchen at his bar cooks something, and I thought, "Damn, are you comparing this place to Jiro?" This was supposed to be when the hook up begins, but it sure as hell didn't feel like it. I'm not picking up on drinking and eating vibes from 'Ole Nick, the best bartender in the world.

Josh continued to harp on his podcast, and his vision for diversity in opinions.

J: You know, Matt and Toby and Joey's...its a good show, but they all pretty much believe the same thing. It sets a very narrow demographic of Christians who like, think the church is annoying. You know those people, it's like, not my people. I get it. But I was there in high school. I went through that phase so long ago, it's like I'm not interested. I'm interested in actually showing community with people who will never believe what I believe. I want to show that I have friendship with these people.

After we spent another 45 minutes chatting about

other members of the band, I needed to take a piss, so I head to the bathroom. The check had just been presented to us as I was getting up. I was skeptical of the hookup from the beginning. Most potential restaurant hookups never work out. They stress me out, really. I would just rather know what to order based on the idea that I'm the one paying for it. Because honestly, we went all out at this place. We ordered multiple courses of food, many many drinks and cocktails. Josh made it seem like it was all good. Nick had us covered.

When I was returning from the bathroom, Josh was closing the booklet that contained the bill and I asked if he had paid. He graciously said something to the tune of "Yeah dude! You're in my town, gotta take care of you." Josh then left to go to the bathroom. I picked up the bill to take a peak. It was large. There was most definitely not a Nick hook up. Now I'm sitting there wondering if Josh paid only because he is a nice guy, or if he also was just embarrassed that his Kramer status did nothing for us. I felt even worse because had I known, I would have just paid. I had a (small) BadChristian budget for this stuff. Oh well.

A: I got a lot of good stuff here. I don't know what else to really ask you.

I ponder for a moment.

A: Well, what's the most fucked up thing you can tell me.

J: Like, about Emery?

A: Yeah. What's the most fucked up thing that ever happened. Just something you would really hate for me to print.

J: Well, we didn't get too crazy you know.

A: Yeah, I know.

J: I mean there might be stuff I don't want my mom to know, but…

A: Yeah.

J: Well…we drew Swastikas on Dave's forehead one time.

A: Thank You. Thank you so much for that.

J: I have tried cocaine twice; did not like it.

A: Really? When?

J: Both recently; both within the last two years; one line each time; both parties; both chill parties.

I don't know why cocaine use shocks me, but every time I hear about a friend using, it just seems insane. However, if I used drugs, I think cocaine goes to the top of the list of drugs to try. Looks fun.

J: I'm gonna try mushrooms sometime. You can put that in the book.

For all the inward dishonesty that Josh burdens himself with, the dude at least gave me the skinny on his drug use. I must respect him for that. That night, I slept in wet clothes on a cold hardwood floor in Josh's bedroom. A room that doubles as his studio. A studio that still has not produced a solo record or a podcast.

10

THE WEAK'S END

Emery did something that not many bands did at that time. They independently paid for a quality record made by a real producer. They had no label help; no label prospects, really. Nowadays, it's really easy and cheap to get a quality record made without the help of a label. Back then, it just wasn't done.

I think Emery figured out that forcing the label to speculate based on demos is a narrow path to success. It was like Major League Baseball teams drafting prospects out of high school. The players are raw. Some players look enticing, but you don't really know how it's going to go. Most guys never see the Major Leagues. According to

Baseball America, only 17.2% of all drafted players from 1987-2008 ever made it to the big leagues. That number includes a lot of guys who only got a "cup of coffee" stint in the Majors. Only 5.5% of those that were drafted play at least three years in the big leagues.

And so it is for labels and bands alike trying to find success in this business. The demo tells you some things about a band. But you don't know how great a band is going to be until you get them in with a good producer, polish up the songs and get a good mix. You could get to the end of that process having dropped fifteen, twenty, thirty thousand dollars to be like, "Well fuck, this record isn't that great. It could tank." This happens all the time. Before Semisonic had their big hit with "Closing Time", their label had lost more than a million dollars promoting the previous record.

Bands like Emery make it easier for everyone. No, making a good record before getting signed doesn't guarantee that people will buy it. But the speculation risk decreases. The people at the label can at least hear a finished record and know what the band sounds like at their best. The whole spotting a diamond in the rough thing goes out the window. All they have to do is figure out how in the hell to sell it to people.

It worked out well for both Emery and my band, As Cities Burn. Like many bands, As Cities Burn burned out touring nonstop before we signed and recorded a real record. Once we got signed we couldn't hold the band together. Emery made smart choices and made it easy for people to want to take a risk on them. Although, there is never any guarantee that a debut record will launch a career such as Emery's, no matter who records it or how good the songs are. Luck plays a part, even when you do the work the way it should be done and try really hard. You have to get lucky too. Emery got lucky.

****

"The Weak's End" writing process? Awesome. Best thing in the universe."

So Matt had a great time with this project. The band planned out six months for finishing the songs for the record, tweaking and perfecting every aspect. They were still on the communal living plan that I described in chapter eight. At the end of the six months, they would go record a real record with somebody. They didn't know who they would record with yet, but their goal was to be ready.

The guys would practice every night. It was like musical chairs of creativity. If someone was home, they would be working on the record. Guys might be at work while others had a night off and they would just do whatever they could to make progress. Once they started getting some music laid out, Toby and Devin would get sent off to work on lyrics, melodies, harmonies, switching vocals, etc. As Matt put it, he would, "arrange the ship," also known in songwriting as...arranging.

"It would just be me and Joel and Seth, and Seth wasn't any good. Joel was good, but he wasn't really with it on the genre. He was a blues guitarist on bass." Basically, Matt micro managed the shit out of the writing process. In his head, he could see where everything needed to go. Think "The Matrix." Someone like Matt is crucial to the record development process. Somebody has to take control and have the vision when putting together songs. If someone fights back, great; even better for the process.

"I would say, 'Ok Seth, you have to start this fill with your left hand 'cause you play open.' I'm sure they thought I was crazy, but we did it." Matt was able to put the insecurity of feeling like the control freak out of his mind and unabashedly be the control freak. It wasn't the best way to go about it, but it was a way to get it done. "It was not efficient at all. I was using them to achieve, to experiment. Seth didn't like to have to be babysat. He was uncomfortable to have to be accountable for each beat within a fill. Toby would say, 'That doesn't work,' then we would fight about that. He would say, 'But I don't want to sing there.' Everything was riding on these songs being finished and I thought every note, beat, hit, melody had to be as good as it could be."

They were still playing shows during this time, too. I think that's a really good thing to do while you are writing songs. It's good to get a sense of how they play on a stage in front of people. Call it market research. I always make changes to drum parts after I've played them live. I'm not sure if Seth was allowed to do so, based on Matt's description of the writing process. Another example of why I could have never got along as a member of Emery.

For their plan to work, Emery needed to find a good producer to take on the project. More important than being good, he (or she, but it's a pretty male-dominated field) had to be established. There needed to be a name attached that would catch the eyes of label people. I don't think at the time Emery probably knew a ton about record producers. In fact, it seems that the list of producers to target only included one person. Matt made contact.

"We emailed the only person we had ever wanted to record with, Ed Rose. Son of a bitch, he wrote us back."

*****

I think it is very fair and appropriate to refer to Ed Rose as a legendary producer, at least in the scene that I grew up caring about. He worked out of Lawrence, Kansas, a college town where the University of Kansas is pretty much the only thing going on in. But there is a vibrant downtown ethnic restaurants, burger joints, and bars. Lawrence also has great music venues, including one of my personal favorites, The Bottleneck. I don't mean to brag, but there is something incredible about playing on a stage that Nirvana also graced in their early years. Only 30 minutes west of Kansas City, it's where most bands play instead of Kansas City. Playing Kansas City sucks. Playing Lawrence fucking rules. Actually, I can't think of a better place to recruit bands for a studio. There's little competition, and an inspirational small-time vibe.

Ed's discography is impressive. Before working with Emery, Ed produced the likes of The Get Up Kids, Motion City Soundtrack, Coalesce, Fuel, Reggie and the Full Effect, Brandtson, The Casket Lottery, The Appleseed Cast, The Beautiful Mistake, and one of my personal favorites, Ultimate Fakebook. More relevant to today's scene, he has worked with Into it. Over it. and Touche Amore.

It was a dream for the Emery dudes to work with Ed, one they never thought would become a reality. But Emery had no clue about the recording business. As a producer, if a decent band is interested in working with you, they have the money, and you aren't George fucking Martin who is too busy working with The Beatles, there is a good chance you will take the job.

I spoke to Ed about Emery, hoping to get a little insight into the project. Understandably, he wasn't aware of the band at all before they contacted him. Nobody was.

I asked him what inclined him to say yes to recording Emery. Did he need the work? Did he think they were actually good?

"It was a little bit of both. You know we had just bought the studio, so getting bodies in the door was important. I think from talking to the guys in the band they seemed like good dudes, and the demos were pretty close. And given the amount of time they had to get the record done, I thought, if they came in really prepared we could pull it off." When Ed says that the demos were "pretty close," he meant that the songs were far enough along to begin tracking. It wasn't going to be surgery in the studio to try and make the songs good. They only had ten days to do the record. That was all they could afford. Ed was $600 per day. Matt fronted half the money for the recording with some investment money he had saved.

"They all tried to save money for the recording, but nobody did a good job, so Matt took out some money," Josh told me. Josh wasn't saving money because he wasn't officially in the band yet. His girlfriend – the infamous Elaine – had just broken up with him and he was really depressed, so the guys asked if he wanted to tag along. But instead he just sat there for ten days and didn't do a damn thing. Matt had no idea if ten days was a lot of time or not. Like I said, they didn't know anything about recording. "I knew everything had to be good and I still didn't think it would be near good enough. There was still lots of stuff that was not good and we trimmed it down, and Ed Rose would say, 'Chop this, chop this, chop this.'"

They went in there with some really long songs. Bands do shit like this. They tend to think everyone is just as interested in their jams as they are. Ed Rose had thoughts on this phenomenon, "Let's say a part goes on eight times…the dudes in the band think 'Wow this is really fun!' Nobody else thinks that's fun. A lot of it was, 'This is probably a lot of fun to play, but honestly, to the average listener, this part is too long.'"

This is the greatest challenge a producer faces when working with a band that is making their first record. Communicating to them that in fact their songs are not perfect and maybe they hired a producer for a reason. Ed praised Emery for their attitude throughout the process. He acknowledged that the genre wasn't really his thing, but he approached it with the goal of making it the best it could be. If the band could get on board with that goal, the record would be successful.

"It all sounded like the stuff of the time. They weren't reinventing the wheel. They seemed really open to making changes to arrangements; showed me they were open minded." Emery was wise to take direction from somebody with experience. Ed's philosophies rubbed off on them. Matt remembered the changes they made to "Walls".

"We added a bunch of screaming. Like, the whole beginning of Walls didn't have any screaming. It was just instrumental. We added the screaming in the studio at the end of the recording. Toby was like, 'Well, it's probably too long without vocals.'" Go listen to that song and try to imagine it without the screaming vocals at the beginning. Thank God they made the change, because I'm serious when I say maybe Emery never gets off the ground without that crucial change.

Ed wasn't phased by the prospect of making the record in ten days. He had made records in ninety minutes in the past. You do what you can with the time you have. Emery was competent enough on their instruments to do the work in the allotted time period. "They could all play. I don't think they had a ton of recording experience, but if they would have sucked we would have never got the record done."

You could say the rest is history. It was such a short amount of time in the studio that there was no time for anything interesting to really happen. The guys weren't really sure if Ed even liked them...like as humans. "He didn't care if we liked him; didn't care if we got along," Josh told me. I know Josh didn't play on the record, but maybe that put him in the interesting position to observe in a way that nobody else that was tied up in making the record was. "He was like, 'I gotta get this work done. My name's on it. It better sound good.'"

I asked Ed if he had listened to the record since he had made it. If there was anything he would have changed. "Honestly, no, since it left the studio. I really hadn't even listened to the completed version until Matt asked me to be on his podcast. I figured I had better brush up on it. I still think it's a good record. I think it turned out great." It's not uncommon for producers to not revisit their work. The work is being done as it's being recorded. Once they finish and deliver a satisfactory product to the band, it's not useful to them anymore. Ed maintains an incredible selflessness even towards those records of his that went on to commercial success. "It's always nice when something you work on does well. But more than anything, I'm just happy for those guys in that band."

"The Weak's End" actually left Ed's studio slightly unfinished. After all the tracks were recorded and produced, Ed was supposed to do a rough mix for the guys to use for shopping the record. However, they had run out of time. At the end of their final day in studio, Ed had completed some mixing. Still unmixed Emery was leaving in the morning and they were anxious to have a fully "rough mixed" record to listen to on the way back to Seattle from Kansas.

"Well, I don't know if I should say this. Ed almost got through the whole record. There was [sic] two songs left. He recorded on Pro Tools. I knew Pro Tools, and I also was kind of familiar with the console he was on. So, in the middle of the night, me and Matt went downstairs and mixed two of the songs on his gear. It was expressly against his rules to touch his shit."

As far as Josh knows, Ed is not aware of this event. I pussied out and didn't even bringing it up in my interview with Ed. J.R. McNeely, who mixed many Tooth and Nail records, would eventually provide a more thorough mixing of the record when Tooth and Nail picked it up, but we are getting a little ahead of ourselves… It's a shame he never got to record Dave Powell on drums. It was probably less editing than Seth required on "The Weak's End".

11

A FEW WORDS ON CHOPPER

Joel Green was supposed to be the

Pandora's box of stories for this book. Matt had been talking for months about how I just needed to hit up Joel and I would get so much good material for the book. Matt thought I could probably write a whole book just based off the journals that Joel kept back when Emery had first started. Boy was he wrong. "When I moved back from Indianapolis, I lost one box. I know it had my record player in it." This is all Joel had to say on the matter of those journals. He figured it must have been in that box.

"Over the years, every time I can't find something, I think it must be in that box." So now I had to actually do real research and make sure I could pull out enough interesting content from all these interviews. Even more so it's made it incredibly difficult to figure out what angle to take with Joel's chapter. Once again – and I know this is getting boring to hear – I really like Joel. I don't think that was always the case, but after getting to know him a little better when I was tour managing Emery I decided that he is a delightful person to be around. Hold up, I have to clarify that scenario. Joel wasn't in the band when I tour managed Emery. Instead, he *worked* for the band for a brief period of time when I tour managed Emery. Since I was the tour manager, I also knew how much he was getting paid, and it was not much at all. I wasn't getting paid much either, but I'm not one to complain about pay. It's not slavery after all. Plus there was always beer. Joel definitely got his fair share of the alcohol. During multiple nights on that tour, I witnessed Joel pass out drunk sitting up in a seat on the bus. Often he wouldn't make it to his bed until very early in the morning. I often had to wake him up to load in, possibly still drunk from the night before. All this makes me very excited to tell you that Joel is sober now. I was very glad to hear so when I chatted with him.

That time he spent on tour when I was Emery's TM seemed to be a rough patch for Joel. I can't imagine what it's like to load in and set up the gear for a band that you were practically an original member of. I guess you just drink and let it all go. Fuck it. As Matt said, "Working for your former band…that's just the shittiest. 'I fucked this up and now I work for them.' But on the other hand, he's Joel. He's cool. He's fun. It wasn't bad."

Even though Joel was a part of the band from the beginning, I feel like it was never a perfect fit. I mean, yes, he had known Toby since they were kids and he was from the same town as all the guys. But he definitely didn't have the look. And if you ever saw him on stage it was well, interesting.

One time I saw Joel play offstage. Let me explain. As Cities Burn did a tour with Emery right after "The Question" came out. Gym Class Heroes and Gatsby's American Dream were also on that tour. It was great. The tour stopped through Houston at a venue that I believe was called Java Jazz. I loved that venue. It was small, but kids always showed up. Almost every show I ever played there was sold out. The stage was small. Like, it barely had enough room for a band to actually fit on the stage. Emery was a six-piece band in those days. They were running in-ear monitors and had all sorts of gear. It was a mess. There was no way they could fit everything on stage. I walked in the venue during their set into the backstage area that doubled as a green room. There was a curtain separating onstage from off. Sitting just outside that curtain was Joel, on a stool, with a microphone on a boom stand and his bass resting on his knee like it was a blues jam session in his buddy's basement. Except Emery was playing a sold out show in support of a record that would go on to sell almost two-hundred-thousand copies. Joel looked way more satisfied than I had ever seen him on stage. He was sitting, after all, and nobody could see him. It was the perfect situation for a person who in all actuality is an extremely talented blues musician. Just, maybe not the showman Emery required.

Joel remembered back to the night Joey mailed his infamous letter to Toby, quitting Emery before they moved to Seattle. "We went to the WOW Wings that night. We were sitting there just eating, having some beers and stuff. Toby was, like, destroyed. Hollowed.

You could tell somebody knocked the air out of him." I can picture Joel sitting there, listening to Toby wallow in the heartbreak of his best friend bailing on him. I can picture Joel wondering why nobody has suggested what to him seemed obvious.

"Why don't I play bass?"

"It was weird to me that nobody thought of that beforehand." I suppose I could think of a few reasons why, but the guys obviously liked the idea enough to go through with it. Joel was already moving with them anyway, just for the hell of it. "I wasn't really going out there with any plan or itinerary or anything. At that time, I was playing a lot blues. I was planning on putting together a blues band out in [Seattle]." I would assume that there is a lack of quality blues bands in Seattle. Maybe Chopper was onto something.

So Joel played in Emery. The blues guitarist played bass in a screamo band. It didn't last. Of course it didn't last.

*****

I asked Matt what finally lead to them kicking Joel

out of the band for good? Matt was direct, but slightly vague on the details. "We were able to fire him on moral grounds, and glad to have that excuse because of how poor and lazy of a worker and partner he was. That's the bottom line. We didn't enjoy being business partners with a guy that I love as a person and a friend. He didn't share the work ethic, and the flexibility, and the ability to be criticized or accountable. And he's lazy. Pathologically lazy." Ouch.

I feel awful even now as I write this. I don't want to hurt anyone. But I want to get to the truth. Discretion is important to me. If Joel was still in the band, I might not include Matt's words.

"Also, on top of that, he was not handling the success and the morality part well, so we were able to...so that was what allowed us to have more reasonable grounds to part ways. We don't say it that way [publicly], but that's the truth." I get back into asking Matt about what it was like having Joel work for Emery. "He's a machine. He's a very bizarre machine, but he's a machine. He compartmentalizes. He's able to separate stuff and operate mechanically. But the outcome result to me is that he suffers from anxiety and stuff. He can handle it, like he can totally handle it." The suppression of these anxieties have their price according to Matt. "He'll be in his room a month after tour and having panic attacks. 'I'm not gonna be sad because my girlfriend dumped me' he definitely can mechanically shut that off, but it comes at a cost."

I sympathize with anyone that struggles with this sort of thing. I struggle with this sort of thing. It can be hard to be open about it with people that don't understand or recognize the validity of it. I think Matt is a lot better these days at showcasing sympathy/empathy than maybe he used to be. But Matt's words on Joel aren't just criticism. The tone in his voice is of concern. I think it breaks his heart. He does love Chopper. "He has a lot of self loathing. He's self destructive, like when he would start drinking a bottle of vodka at three in the morning, that's not anything other than to punish yourself. That whole phase for him, was 'Fuck Joel' and 'Punish Joel.' That's the whole cycle he's been in for years since he left the band. He's getting out of it maybe now. It's positive he's sober and he's working out." Matt went on talking about when Joel was still in the band. "He was like doing stuff like trying to hit on the ugliest girl in the bar and telling stories like 'I would just get in the elevator with the people in my building and I'd fart and don't react and see what happens.' That's like…that's not funny. It's funny that you would do it and say it, but it's self destructive. I don't know if it's a cry for help. Working for your former band…that's just the shittiest. 'I fucked this up and now I work for them.' But on the other hand, he's Joel. He's cool. He's fun. It wasn't bad."

I was almost done writing this book – on the last day before turning in my first draft for edit notes – when I tuned into the latest episode of the BadChristian Podcast. Toby had found an email chain that was written between he, Devin, and Matt. They were going back and forth about how to go about firing Chopper. Devin wrote the "copy" for what he proposed they send; emphasis on *send* not *say* to Joel. Yes, at this point it was the plan to fire Joel via email. See the email from Devin to Matt and Toby below. Also take note of Devin's email address. Love it:

From: "devin   shelton" <<u>imengagedsodontask@hotmail.co</u> <u>m</u>>

Subject: joel-please add to or take away

Date: May 25, 2006 at 12:15:07 PM CDT

To: matt@emerymusic.com, watervsrock@yahoo.com

joel,

we have some things we need to talk to you about. we wanted to be able to talk to you in person, but the distance and time didn't allow for it.

we have been thinking and praying about this for quite a while, and after we talked with you at matt's house in january, we hoped that we would see a significant change in you. unfortunately, we can't say that we have. we appreciate you moving around more on stage at times, but it seems like your mood

affects how you play. we all have bad days, but it is our responsibility to get past that and put on a good show.

since emery began, we have noticed that we have to push you to get things done because your motivation is lacking. that bothers us because we have all worked so hard to get the band where it is now. that's not to say that you haven't done anything for the band, but honestly, it's hard to find any real initiative in you. it's not the easiest thing in the world to come to you with a problem, it is very uncomfortable. but we have tried and tried to make you a part of what we are, and it just seems impossible to draw you closer. we're sorry if you have felt left out in any way, but it's not only our responsibility to make things different, it's yours too.

you truly don't realize how hard this is for us to say because we have been friends for such a long time, but we have to go beyond that and look at emery for what it is...a business. and we feel that it would be best for our business, our band, and you as a person, for you to no longer be a part of it.

we know this will come as somewhat of a shock and like we said, we wish we could have done things differently. for what it's worth, feel free to call any of us to talk about it, but we understand if not. we hope that this doesn't ruin our friendship forever, but we know that it will change things and for that we are sorry. we will miss being around you because you are a very fun-loving guy. we love you as a great, great friend and brother in Christ and will always hold you high in our prayers.

devin, matt, toby, dave, josh

please add or take away anything
needed. this was really hard to write,
so feel free to write better ones. i
just wanted to get started.

devin

But Joel would find the email on Matt's
computer, left sitting open on the bus. I don't know how
in the hell that really happens, and it's incredibly
unfortunate. Obviously, Joel was not happy. It's an
absolutely awful way to find out anything. Poor Chopper.
Things didn't go well for him for awhile after he left
Emery.

*****

Chopper is a strange character. "He
called his band mates: 'Oh yeah I quit the band, I'm
moving to Seattle. I think they actually had a show that
Friday." Seth remembered when Chopper decided to

move west with Emery. This is all in reference to Joel quitting his blues band in South Carolina. He thinks he may have even made that call when they were already on the road to Seattle.

"On tour he got into this thing where he wouldn't wear socks more than once. He would wear them and then throw 'em away." I actually don't think that's super weird. New socks feel amazing. Why would you wear old ones if you didn't have to? Although it's not clear where Chopper's endless supply of socks came from.

"And then, he wouldn't keep any change in his pockets. He would throw away all his change." Seems like he could have kept the change to fund his sock habit... "It was just him being weird or him being weird to be funny 'Oh yeah...I'm not a change guy.'"

Then there was the time Chopper took a taxi to a car dealership. To buy a car. If ever one could signal that you were an easy sales target, just show up to a car dealership in a taxi. I heard about this story from one of the other guys. I think it must have been off tape because I can't find it, but I did remember to bring it up to Chopper.

"I was living with Josh and his brother Caleb. They

had a house out in Maple Valley. I had gotten home from tour but Caleb and Josh were gone for a few days. They didn't tell me and I didn't have a key." Chopper got his lady friend to take him to a Starbucks where he called John Dunn, Emery's A&R at Tooth and Nail. Jon let him stay at his place or a few days. However, Chopper felt that he had no independence.

"The next day I woke up and was sitting at the apartment and I thought. I need to have a car. We were making some money at this point." He had a Honda in high school and thought those were pretty good cars. So he called a taxi and asked to be dropped off at a Honda dealership. "I walked right in the front door, and a dude walked up and said, 'Hey how can I help you today?' And I said, 'Yeah…I need to buy a car. Today." That was that. I wonder how much over sticker price Chopper paid for that Honda.

"I was just couch surfing. No way to get anywhere. And at that point I was like I can continue to couch surf. But I gotta have some wheels."

"You still have that car?" I asked.

"No man. I sold it." I figured he still had it. After all it's a Honda and he mentioned how he thought they were good cars. "I sold it to this kid. He was the son of my mom's friend. I sold it to him for like eight hundred bucks." Either Joel is a bad salesmen or Honda's are a God awful investment. Anyways, the car didn't make it long with the kid.

"He was driving and pulled out in front of guy. Got t-boned and the car got totaled. It's in a heap of trash now." A sad ending to the "Chopper takes a taxi to the Honda dealership" saga. I'm searching. I'm struggling. I am trying to pull something out of Joel. Trying desperately to tap into the memories of these lost journals. We had been talking for about thirty minutes, but I was still unsatisfied. I needed to tap into the fountain of information that had been teased to me by Matt.

"Is there anything else you can remember? Any stories or things that might have happened that would be interesting to talk about?"

"Ummm. Hmmm. I don't know. Man, I guess I'm gonna have to think about that. Yeah…"

"Ah yeah dude it's all good. Matt was just saying you would have a lot of stories." I didn't want to make him feel bad about under delivering on potential entertainment. I figured we would hash it out for another hour or so. See if anything came up. Joel abruptly stopped me mid sentence.

"As a matter of fact I'm gonna have to split, I got some dinner with my friends."

"Oh…Ok man no problem. We can talk again later."

We never did. Because that's just too perfect a way to end a chapter about Joel. I'm just going to leave it at that.

12

DAVE POWELL

If you've ever had the pleasure of forcing your way onto Emery's bus in an awkward and intrusive fashion - of course I'm speaking to weird fans right now - then you probably would have seen Dave sitting in the back corner of the lounge, drum pad on his lap, practicing rudiments, and enjoying whatever shitty light beer Matt and Toby have decided to like for that tour. There Dave will sit, observing and analyzing the situation at hand, deciding how uncomfortable or anxious he may feel about whatever events may be transpiring on the Emery bus. Dave is a strange and uncomfortable fella. But do not underestimate Dave Powell. He has made more progress in his personal and spiritual life than any single member of the band Emery. Also, he isn't as timid as he appears to be.

"You've seen Dave when he's drunk or confrontational. Have you heard about it?" Matt asked. "He can be confrontational especially with strangers. I think it's the flip side of being timid and being a people pleaser. It's the thing where you snap and that comes out." Matt told me how a bouncer at a show got in Dave's space about something and Dave snapped. "Do you know who I am?" and got right in his face. The bouncer backed off. Dave will just act absolutely insane and people back off. Once he was letting his wife Laura off out front of a Walmart when she was really pregnant and an off duty cop came up and started barking at him. Dave went off on the cop. The cop didn't do a damn thing.

In Vegas, walking down the strip, some bro made fun of something somebody in the Emery entourage was wearing. Dave walked up to the guy, and slapped him in the face. "Hey. Fartboy. Get out of here." Slaps him again and the guy retreated.

On Warped Tour, Dave went into the shower trailer with Laura because she didn't feel safe going in alone.

The lines are always long for these things with bands and tour personnel waiting to shower. When Dave and his wife walked out of the shower trailer, some Warped Tour crew guy started yelling at Dave about how it's not cool he is using the shower to get pussy. Dave went into do-you-know-who-I-am mode again. "I play drums in Emery. This is my wife. She didn't want to get raped." Emery was in their heyday when this one went down. The crew guy apologized and I'm pretty sure Dave might have even had Emery's TM complain to Kevin Lyman, the founder of Warped.

Dave has even confronted me about this book. I interviewed him at his office near downtown Indianapolis. He does SEO marketing and makes more money than anybody else in Emery these days. We were drinking beers, talking about his years before Emery and how he joined the band. Dave mentioned that he'd read over the sample chapter I'd written for my BC proposal. But even though my intention is to write an origins-type book (which unfortunately doesn't include him in the timeline), he wasn't having it. The conversation went like this.

D: This is something that if I don't tell you, I think it will bug me later.

A: No, I understand.

D: I don't ever speak up on things like this.

A: The night I was writing it was strictly like, "Ok this is going to be an origin story."

D: I don't really care. No. No. I *will* care. Do I really care? No. But I'm saying I am Emery's drummer. I've been Emery's drummer since September 2004. At this point, I have almost 12 years invested in the band. And you look at Seth and he has two or three years. It's not even like a competition. But I'm thinking, 'If Josh is in the main intro, and I'm not. It's just not right.'"

Dave was laughing, but he was also serious.

D: I'll put that on you. You fix it. Or not.

*****

Dave grew up in Carmel, Indiana. It's a white flight town. Actually, maybe it's not. Indianapolis has to be one of the whitest places on earth. Anyways, it's a nice suburban place to grow up. Dave was kind of a "bad kid", actually. Drugs, alcohol, theft. Dave told me that while in high school band, he would steal cymbals, hardware, whatever he could. He wasn't even trying to be sneaky, either. He'd just steal things, walk right through the school out the door, and never bring it back. Dave isn't dumb, but I don't think he did well in school. It just wasn't for him.

Dave's brother was responsible for getting him into music. It started with Motley Crue. That was Dave's first favorite band and he loved Tommy Lee. I wish I could say – as a drummer – that Tommy Lee was my favorite drummer as a kid. It's so predictable, but it's so right. Tommy Lee is the quintessential rock star drummer and your kid should be so lucky to idolize him in their formative years. Later, Dave got into Zao, and started following the hardcore and punk bands of Tooth Nail in the late nineties. We didn't talk about it specifically in this interview, but I know from other conversations with

Dave that Dave Grohl and Taylor Hawkins are major influences on Dave's drumming, too. We have discussed influences at length while on tour with each other, and it's damn obvious to a drummer that Grohl and Hawkins have infiltrated Dave's style.

Dave hits drums as hard as any drummer I've ever known. For all the confidence Dave has historically lacked in his daily interactions with the world (his ability to confront me is a testament to how he's changing), he makes up for it behind the drum kit. Dave is the man. He's an amazing drummer. He is the single most talented member of Emery in terms of mastery over their respective instrument. Nobody in Emery is better at what they do than Dave is at drums. He could play for anybody. Dave ought to be living in Nashville or LA playing for Kelly Clarkson or Keith Urban or something. Hell, he could step in for Taylor Hawkins in the Foo Fighters, and nobody would ever notice except for the fact that Dave might not look as good in a dress as Taylor Hawkins. Dave cares about playing drums in a way I never have. He practices. He learns rudiments. He talks about drumming. He watches drum videos. The dude cares.

Dave was playing for a band called Bowels of Judas when Emery came knocking. Bowels had done some touring, but the band was stagnating. There is this guy in Indianapolis named Mark LaFay. He was a promoter and band manager. A couple of his bands did pretty well - Haste the Day and Still Remains. I've been aware of Mark since before As Cities Burn was signed. He had a reputation. He still has a reputation. But, it's evolved over the years from cutthroat manager to guy that cures meat in his basement and wins BBQ competitions in Indiana, which is fucking worthless if you ask me. I tend to think that people in Indiana don't know shit about BBQ, but that's a different book.

Mark called Dave and said, 'Hey, you need to go try out for this band Emery.' Seth had quit, and they were trying out different drummers. Mark was in the loop with the Tooth and Nail world because of Haste the Day. He basically vouched for Dave. Emery had a tour coming up, and that would be his audition. However, Dave did not want to do it.

"So I got a call from Mark Lafay. The Bowels of Judas, we were just playing some local stuff. I was working for Caterpillar machinery. I got a call from Mark about joining Emery for one tour. I had to fly out to Seattle. I was petrified of flying. I'd never flown before. I talked to Matt on the phone."

Remember when I wrote that I don't negotiate with Matt on the phone?

"What was that conversation like?"

"Same way it would be now. Matt definitely put off the vibe like he's not super interested in me. I don't know if that was manipulative. Matt's really good at controlling situations, or whatever, and I mean that in a good way. He had me pretty good. I thought, 'This guy doesn't seem interested in me at all, and it seems like a good opportunity.'"

Matt told him to book a plane ticket out to Seattle and the band would reimburse him. "That alone scared me to death more than even flying. I was like, 'Wait, I have to use a credit card and get on the computer?' I didn't even know how to do that. That was in 2004."

Dave wouldn't have done it if not for his wife, Laura.

"I talked to her about it and she was, like, really encouraging me to do it. I was nineteen. She was 18. I think she had just graduated. She convinced me to do it. I was almost trying to tell her to talk me out of it. At the time my anxiety was kind of at a peak anyways, due to drug use." Dave was into the weed.

So because of Laura, Emery got their drummer, it seems.

"I had to go join this band with these guys that were southern. I didn't really like the music. I had to learn the songs 'cause I wanted to make sure they were good, all this stuff. Laura talked me into doing it. Thank God she did."

*****

I mentioned earlier in the chapter that Dave has progressed as a person more than anybody in this band. Emery challenged him to grow. He embraced all the opportunities presented to him since then and that has made all the difference.

From Matt's perspective, "He's learning how to be assertive. That's an admirable quality, to learn how to change how you are. Dave's just running his family good, running a business, playing the drums, physically fit, becoming assertive, learning skills. He just realizes you can do that. You don't have to accept what you thought you were. He's totally, literally, decided to change that. Toby's the way he is. I'm the way I am. Dave has decided to change the way he is. I mean, it's really admirable."

Matt and Toby were kind of like older brothers to Dave. They would give him a hard time, tease him like siblings do, all in hopes that maybe he would end up better for it. It didn't always work the way they wanted, but Dave seems to have changed for the better.

"True friendship for adult males, I think, is really important. The reason I talk about that is that's a big thing I learned from Emery, probably the most important thing is adult male friendship."

It makes me really happy that Dave has come to realize the value of comradery, dudes being dudes. Being open and honest with a group of men is important in the development of manhood, and I truly believe contributes to being a better husband and father. I've often wondered how different Dave's life could have been without Emery. Maybe he would have never married Laura. Maybe he would have just kept working for Caterpillar, smoking weed and drinking a twelve pack of Miller Light everyday after work, living a shitty life. I'm just so happy that I can say that Dave is the shit and has a great family.

A: I feel bad now. I feel bad because you're right and I didn't even…I wasn't even thinking of it in terms of like this is the band. I was thinking of it in terms of a story arc that I was pitching.

D: I think it's really good.

A: I hope you'll be pleased with your mark on the book.

D: I'll say this. Being thirty now and having kids, I'm realizing it's just better to be more forward about things. Same thing with writing. I didn't write a lot on other records. And I told Matt with this next record I'm going to spend a lot of time in my basement writing drum parts and making them the best that they can be. In the early years, I didn't write a lot because I thought I couldn't. There were times that conversations would come up, and I feel like I deserve credit for something, and I would just back down.

A: Since you weren't an original member, it automatically puts you on the fringe even though you are the drummer, and a great drummer. The only good drummer Emery's ever had. So anytime I'm talking to these guys about how Emery got started, no matter what, you don't even come into the picture until "The Question." And that's when the band got the biggest.

D: I like to think I had some part in it. Maybe I didn't....

Of course he did. Dave made Emery sound good. That's what good drummers do.

[13]

The Nail

Does Tooth and Nail Records really need much of an introduction? This is a situation where I feel like if you really don't know anything about this record label, maybe go watch their documentary or just read a Wikipedia page. This isn't a book on the history and success of Tooth and Nail. The long story short is that a guy named Brandon Ebel started a punk rock label and then signed a shit ton of bands and sold a shit ton of records; bands like MxPx, Slickshoes, Further Seems Forever, The Juliana Theory, Living Sacrifice, Anberlin, Underoath, Norma Jean, and on and on and on. It's a pretty kick ass label, and it's a label that I dreamt of being on from the time I was sixteen years old. I fulfilled that dream at twenty years old when, as many of you reading already know, my band As Cities Burn inked a deal with this Seattle-based institution.

So the question is, did Emery move to Seattle just for Tooth and Nail? They say not really. They liked a lot of Tooth and Nail bands, but they swear that it was just a far away place that sounded cool. Plus, they liked grunge music. As Seth told me, "Grunge definitely influenced the move."

Based on my conversations, I believe that they didn't explicitly have any aspirations to stalk out some Tooth and Nail people and figure out a way to get a record deal. Nevertheless, that's exactly what happened. They befriended a guy – well at the time he was almost still a kid – that would play a huge role in getting Emery's career going, Jonathan Dunn.

I spoke with Jon via Skype to get his side of the story on all of this. "So I knew Josh Head from probably when we were like fifteen years old. We ended up going to the same youth group together." Jon and Josh played in the worship band together at church as well as messing around with other local band- type stuff. Jon got himself pretty involved in local music around Seattle.

Josh had told Jon about these weird southern dudes that had started working at Guitar Center with him who had left everything behind to move all the way out to Seattle to start a band. I guess Josh thought maybe Jon was a good guy for Emery to get a foot in the door with the local scene. Jon recalls being impressed. "Super gung-ho. No doubt of their drive and their hunger to pull this shit off. 'We will quit all our jobs tomorrow if we can just go on tour.'" So Jon and the members of Emery became friends. Jon said he started helping them get some of their local shows by introducing them to people he knew. Jon's tone wasn't at all braggadocios about Emery's eventual success ad his role in it. Jon is just a dude who knew his way around Seattle. He was happy to do it. The same as anyone who gets to know Emery, he really liked the guys, and was entertained by their shenanigans and accents. Every time Jon would try and quote someone in the band, he ventured into this awful southern redneck impression. I didn't call him out on it. I'm married to a west coast girl. I love hearing those folks try and sound like us southerners.

When Emery started getting out and touring, one of

the first tours they did – if not *the* first – was with a band that Jon was in. He had booked a bunch of shows for his band and another. The other band dropped off last minute and so Jon figured he'd ask Emery to go. "You have 3 days to figure out if you can do it," Jon told them. They did. They got shifts covered and hit the road. They would have just quit their jobs if they had to.

The day that Jon got home from that tour, Tooth and Nail called and asked if he wanted to come work in the mail room. Back then, the label was still doing tons of mail order business. You had twenty-year old kids holed away on the bottom floor of the Tooth and Nail office just stuffing envelopes all day with CD's, shirts, stickers, skate decks, etc. I've visited this mail room and looted my fair share of goods, including a SICK Further Seems Forever track jacket. The typical scene in the mail room involved people blasting music, not paying any attention to anybody that walked through. Hell, the people walking through probably weren't paying any attention to them either. It was the have's and have not's. But you had to go through the mail room to get upstairs to the main offices.

Around the time that Dunn started working at The

Nail, Emery was going in with Ed Rose to record "The Weak's End". As Jon tells it, he remembers hearing their demos, going to their early shows, and thinking how long and boring the songs were. "Walls" was eight minutes long when they first wrote it. After they finished the record with Ed, as Jon remembers it, they sent him a CD-R before they even got back to Seattle. Talking to the band, it seemed like Jon was kind of soliciting them to let him have a copy to take into the office. The band was reluctant. As Devin put it, "We knew Jon worked in the mail room. He had no pull."

It's true. He was just a scrub. He had been pitching all sorts of bands and trying to get people to listen to demos he had brought in. But nothing was getting through. "I don't even think Brandon knew my name," Jon told me. Regardless, Jon got the CD, brought it into his office and put it on the stereo. Loud.

"Walls" was the first track. "I threw it in, and started shoving an envelope, and my jaw just hit the floor. What I heard on that CD was not the same dudes. This was otherworldly within the context." Jon said he just put the song on repeat. Over and over he played it. "It was like cocaine."

Brandon Ebel, founder, president, and owner of the label came into work as "Walls" was blaring in the mailroom nonstop.

"I walked through the mail room and Jon Dunn was playing "Walls", and I was like, 'who is that?'

Jon responded to Brandon, "I told him, 'Oh this is this band, Emery. They are my friends, looking to sign.'"

"'Well why don't you sign them.' I threw out some numbers and then left the room," says Brandon.

Jon had zero label experience. He didn't really even understand what it meant to sign a band or how to go about it. "I ran it up to director of A&R [Chad Johnson], 'Brandon said I could sign them! What does that mean?!'" Chad gave Jon the rundown essentially of how to become an A&R guy and sign a band, what would be typical to offer them, and how to pitch it to Brandon.

Jon left Chad's office, went to Brandon and basically regurgitated whatever Chad told him about record contracts. Jon was overzealous. Before he got too far, Brandon made it clear that he wanted to see the band play live first. Jon was a little deflated, but it was a start. So Jon "booked" Emery.

"They wanted us to come play a show in the Tooth

and Nail basement. Just for them. It was pretty awkward. They were literally like three or four feet in front of us," Devin recalled. Jon said the entire office came down there to watch, about fifteen people in all. The band played two or three songs and then everyone went back to work. How awful!

Jon recalls chasing after Brandon and asking him, "'What do you think? Are you into it?' 'Yeah it's pretty good, but the guys just don't look the part. Kind of overweight, don't dress cool, kind of backwoods.'"

Brandon put it a bit more delicately to me on the phone. "They were kind of quirky, kind of redneck. They had the songs. They had the work ethic."

Devin understood. "Toby was quite a bit overweight, and Joel is kind of the same. I think Brandon didn't like that. I remember Jon - there was something said and kind of took a couple steps back, and we were like, 'holy crap.' I don't think they ever directly said, 'lose weight' but we got the insinuation that we needed to look better.'" It's funny to hear Devin, the good-looking dude that he is, recall the 'too-fat to sign' perception of his band.

Jon says he never explicitly told the guys that

Brandon wanted them to lose weight. Instead, it was their "overall image". "I go [sic] to the band and tried to get them to work on their image." Jon said he even took Matt shopping one day to show him what the cool kids were wearing. If you recall, Matt has never given consideration to the way he looks. In 2003, being in a cool scene band meant buying girl jeans. Skinny jeans weren't on the clothes racks in the men's section yet. So for a guy, it was hard to find jeans that were "fitted". Girl jeans were the only option. The crotches and waistlines were a little weird, but they did the trick. (Oh, yes, I bought girl jeans in 2003 too.)

Jon took Matt to The Express. He tried on some girl jeans. Jon goes into his bad southern accent impression making fun of Matt, "I don't know about this." Jon encouraged him. This is what the kids were doing. Emery wanted to get a record deal, so Matt went along with it. They headed back to Josh's parents house to show off his new wardrobe.

Jon continued, "Matt comes walking in wearing his new pants and everyone starts DYING of laughter, mocking him relentless. Toby was rolling on the floor. 'YOU LOOK LIKE A GOOFBALL MAN!' Matt was like,

'I don't know man, they are pretty comfy.'"

Jon claims the band collectively lost two-hundred-and fifty pounds on the Atkins diet. Brandon never misses an opportunity to express his surprise at their improvement. "Next time I saw them, a couple of them had lost like 60 pounds. I was like WHOA!"

"They looked the part," Jon concluded. "Brandon's like, 'Cool. I think this is worth signing. Here's your first shot to be an A&R guy.'"

Congrats Jon Dunn, you became an A&R guy. But ah, yes…record deals. They are a fucking bitch and they don't just get signed overnight.

*****

Tooth and Nail was not the only label that Emery talked to. After they had finished recording with Ed, Emery was on tour in California, so they decided to drive over to the office for Nitro Records, which was the label The Offspring owned. They knocked on the door, told them who they were, and offered treats as a gift. They wouldn't take the treats – because, you know, like, people are crazy, and maybe Emery had poisoned them – but the label manager did invite them inside to hang out and talk, and even listened to some of their record. Emery had an entire PA system in the trailer with a generator. They were ready to play anywhere. They offered to set up in the parking lot outside of Nitro records to play a show for them. Nitro politely declined, but did praise Emery's audacity and commitment. By all accounts, the label manager told them that Emery wasn't really their cup of tea, but he wished all his bands worked as hard and cared as much as Emery did.

Not every outrageous attempt at contacting labels was as successful as Emery's encounter with Nitro Records. Seth thought maybe Emery should try and get a demo to Fred Durst. Well, maybe just for shits and giggles. But that didn't stop him from trying.

"One time Seth called Fred Durst," Devin told me. "He called the label and a lady answered. He was like, 'Yeah, Fred Durst please,' and she was like, 'One moment.'" She put the call through. But it went to voicemail. Seth left a message about Emery and ended, according to Devin, "It would *behoove* you to call us back."

I've never heard of a band pitch themselves to just one label. They were definitely making more progress with Tooth and Nail than anywhere else, but even then, Tooth and Nail might not have been their first choice. Victory Records was a big target. All their bands were huge and of the same genre as Emery. They touted the likes of Thursday, Taking Back Sunday, and eventually bands like Hawthorne Heights and A Day to Remember. Victory had something going over there, despite the shady business practices of the label owner, Tony Brummel. This wouldn't come to light for some time, and it resulted in many bands filing lawsuits against the label. Tony called Emery two months after they had already signed with The Nail. "Man, that could have been really good," Devin recalled. "But looking back, probably could have ended up in a lawsuit."

The Militia Group, home to a shit ton of cool bands – Copeland, The Appleseed Cast, Brandtson, Cartel, Rufio, Lovedrug, Acceptance, The Jealous Sound – was also in the mix for Emery. One of the owners of TMG, Chad Pearson, had worked at Tooth and Nail for awhile and then left to set up shop with Rory Felton. They started as a booking agency, and then morphed into a label. I would say, if any label was in direct competition with Tooth and Nail, this was it. As Cities Burn, for instance, had an offer from The Militia Group as well as Tooth and Nail. This was the case with Emery as well. According to Dunn, The Militia Group didn't make their offer until after Tooth and Nail made theirs.

I asked Devin, "Why Tooth and Nail?"

"I don't remember some specific detail about that."

"Was it because Rory was kind of weird?" I asked.

"It had nothing to do with that. I think maybe we thought Tooth and Nail was a little bigger."

According to Josh, Emery's lawyer told them that The Militia Group offer was better than The Nail's, so Emery just went to Tooth and Nail and asked them to match the TMG offer and we will sign. So, that's what happened.

On the phone, I told Brandon about my first impressions of Emery when I saw the video for "Walls". I thought, no way the scene was going to buy this. What the hell is The Nail doing? Brandon fell somewhere in the middle on Emery. I asked him what he projected them to be, just from a professional/label owner viewpoint. "So that's the thing, there are lots of bands I signed that I thought would be huge that weren't. And then there are the bands you don't think will and they do. Emery was probably in between. I thought maybe they were too quirky."

According to Jon, it's a big hurdle to get the entire label behind a release. But he was able to garner support for Emery from two key players at Tooth and Nail, John Frazier and Derek Timbush. John Frazier was the marketing guy at The Nail. Derek Timbush was in charge of sales. Meaning, Derek was the reason you could buy an Emery record at Best Buy. "Without those dudes, we wouldn't be talking about Emery right now. Those guys deserve a shit ton of credit. I was just trying to keep up with those guys." John was let go from Tooth and Nail a couple years ago, and now has his own label. Derek became a professional poker player, of all things.

Record label offices are just like any other office setting. It's tough to get other people to stick their neck out for something you are working on. Nobody wants to be associated with something that fails or loses money for the company. Jon was still working in the mail room while simultaneously doing A&R for Emery, and was putting in sixty-hour work weeks. Jon still had a long way to go. Simply signing a band wasn't that big of a deal at the point. You have to *sell records.*

Emery went on tour. They were on the road non-stop for two years, playing the record and building a fan base. Jon worked his ass off circumventing the system when necessary to pitch Emery to radio, and get them attention from others working at the label. That's essentially an A&R person's job; to advocate for their bands and take advantage of the resources the label has to offer.

"The Weak's End" crushed it. It exceeded every expectation that Brandon had for an overweight group of poorly dressed rednecks. That was a solid investment there, Mr. Ebel.

14

MY BEST FRIEND, TOBY

Once while I was tour managing Emery, Toby

accused me of not giving him his per diem. For those not

in the know, per diem is a cash payout that you get when

you are on tour. Sometimes the per diem is ten dollars a

day, sometimes it's forty. It just depends on what the

band wants to do. Essentially it's money you don't have

to tell your wife about. Walking around money for being

on the road. On this particular tour, per diem's for the

band were $100 per week. I would put the cash in an

envelope or wrap it up in a rubber band and place it on

the pillow of the respective band member's bunk. Theft

wasn't even a consideration. I did this so I didn't have to

hold on to a band member's cash in my pocket until I saw them next. Once I subtracted the per diem payments from my cash spreadsheet, I wanted the money off of my person. So I did the bunk cash-drop. This was never a problem. Until one day, Toby got upset. This story is best told by Matt, who claims it's not just a story, it's an examination into Toby's inner being. Matt believes the per diem story reveals everything about Toby you need to know. Previously, as in Josh's chapter, I've let the band member speak for himself. But in this case, I've chosen to flip the script and let everyone else speak about Toby. I will make it through this entire fucking book without attributing a single fucking quote to Toby. This is art.

MATT: He doesn't lose stuff very much. He thinks he loses stuff everyday. He thinks he loses his wallet everyday and then he finds it somewhere later. The other bias is that you never have as much money in your wallet as you think you do. And he thinks he loses stuff everyday and you're sure you gave it to him.

Toby was INSISTING that the band give him his per diem because he INSISTED that I either lost it or never gave it to him.

MATT: Everybody would have caved but me. Josh would never say anything. Dave would think that he was wrong, but let him have a hundred dollars. If it wasn't for me, you were working for him…you would have given him another hundred dollars, of course. So that's just me being a dickhead, but I know I was right.

MATT: Don't I have to have some principle somewhere? I don't care about a hundred dollars either, but at some point, I have to have some principle somewhere. I think most people's best qualities are also their worst qualities. And so it may be a function of Toby's actual creativity, which I can't say enough good stuff about. He literally thinks of something and then forces it to be a reality, period. And he is willing to be blind in whatever way he needs to, or defy logic and stuff. It's a really strong quality. It's the opposite of Josh. Instead of ignoring reality, he can cause something. That's what creating is, causing something to come into existence by sheer will power. He just will do that. Half the time it's just real stupid stuff, like [the per diem]. And then the other realm of that is, 'I'm writing a song. This is good. No, this is my voice. I'm playing this note over that chord.' And then I go, 'Holy shit he sang *that* note over *that* chord, that's not even right. It's just unbelievable. Imposing of your will into reality. But, that's the same problem he has with thinking he is owed another hundred dollars. He just isn't. I don't think he still thinks about it. But if you bring it up, he'll think, 'Fuck. A hundred dollars I didn't get.' It's not like I'm going to convince him. There's no point where he's like 'Yeah, yeah, I guess I could see that.' It's NOT going that way. It's only gonna go deeper. He'll think of the most creative absurd things possible to reinforce or attack you. That's probably what his main technique would have been. 'But Aaron, you screw up a lot of stuff.' Or, 'Well, how much is this?' Or, 'Where did you put this that time?' Or, 'How good are your spreadsheets?' 'Ok, Ok, Mister Got-His-Good-Spreadsheets over here. Who do you think's better? Aaron with his spreadsheets or me not knowing if I lost a hundred dollars?' And he would just take that to another level. Doubling down is his usual.

MATT: My gosh, most people can't work with him. I

don't know anybody else that can, in a way. I mean, I know people can, I'm not saying, 'Oh ME!' I'm saying it's not easy. Most people couldn't do it. It wouldn't be worth it to most people to work with him. His wife is special. They're a pretty good match. I mean, the girlfriends before, they would throw things at each other and cuss as loud as they could at each other. That's what you would actually expect him to have in a relationship. And somehow Jessica is like the opposite; disarming him and having some kind of control over him. And all his other relationships, it's like him screaming fuck you, and throwing tapes against the wall and breaking. That's what I thought he was always destined to (fail?) in relationships. 'Fuck you, get out of the car!' Leave his girlfriend on the side of the road and drive off. That's the kind of stuff he had in all his previous relationships.

JOSH: You can't argue rationally. You could change subject on him in the middle of an argument and he wouldn't notice. I don't argue with Toby anymore.

MATT: One of the worst arguments we've ever had was [about] which way are [sic] we gonna drive to get to

Seattle when we moved there.

Matt told me to ask my band mate from As Cities Burn, Colin Kimble, about the time Toby shoved a sandwich in his face. I called him up and he had no recollection. When I mentioned I was writing about arguing with Toby, and that Matt had so much to say about working with Toby, Colin simply replied, "To this day, I remain amazed that they are friends."

MATT: We are fine any amount of minutes later. Maybe I'm mad for a few minutes, but definitely not thirty minutes later. Thirty minutes later? The same as yesterday.

AARON: Do you think you'll always be doing something with Toby?

MATT: I think so. I think I'll always do something with Toby.

Matt told me when, back in college, he realized that Toby was his "ticket".

MATT: I'm gonna use this (Toby) and go a really long way. I can do a lot with this. This is like a resource. I realize [sic] I can be of use to him or he could be of use to me. I don't know what it was, but I was like, this is real talent. Something I've never seen before. This is really a valuable thing that I don't think he understood, or knew, or I don't think anybody else did. I'll go all in with this guy. This is it. This outflow of humor and talent and leadership and strength. I'll hitch to this. We can do this.

It's not without challenges. Aside from all of the personality flaws that Toby possesses, you have to get talent moving in the direction you want it to go.

MATT: Toby is like the most powerful mustang stallion in the world and you have no idea which direction he's even gonna want to go. And like, I know where we are trying to go, and if he would go the same direction, it's unbelievable.

But then you are back to the personality flaws.

SETH: I used to do serious pranks. I was cutting metal (working on the bus). I had some ketchup, and I acted like I sliced my fingers off. I think Toby freaked out, but his first thought was, 'What's the band gonna do?' He was only thinking of himself, not the fact that I had cut four fingers off.

*****

I met Toby at a Starbucks on a shitty road west of historic Charleston. I think it was close to the megachurch he was working for at the time. When he showed up, he was decked out in Clemson gear and sweating profusely having just finished a workout. He looked good. I think he said he had lost forty pounds since I had last seen him. I was hungry and I told him that we should go get lunch and do our interview. Being in Charleston, I wanted to get something REAL good. I found a place called Nana's Seafood in a historic neighborhood of Charleston. There were only two tables in the joint. Me and Toby were the only white folk in there during the two hours we ate and interviewed. Before arriving at Nan's, Toby had stressed to me that he was trying to eat low carb and didn't want fried food. Well, this place specializes in steamed crab and shrimp. They call it garlic crab. They steam the blue crabs and then toss them in this amazing mayo based garlic sauce. Same with the shrimp. Just unbelievable. I also ordered us mac and cheese, and perlou with sausage and oysters. Perlou is kind of like jambalaya; so, a bunch of rice, plus the pasta. None of this was low carb. It wasn't until after I left for the airport that I realized I was the only one of us chowing down on all the carbs like the fucking fat ass I am. Toby, probably silently judging me, stuck to his diet.

Nobody gets the benefit of the doubt with Toby. He has never once liked a friend of mine upon first meeting them. Like, if I bring someone on the bus, he instantly believes the person must be shitty. Toby is constantly inquiring who I hang out with; what I do with my time. He squints at me and nods his head a lot. He always seems skeptically concerned.

Toby was present for two of the worst days of my life, the day I broke my femur and the day I had a panic attack in the middle of playing an As Cities Burn show. When I broke my leg, he rode in the van with me to the hospital. He and Matt sat backstage and talked me down from the "ledge", so to speak when I had the panic attack. The best part is that while I know he cares, I also think he gets a great sense of adventure out of watching my life fall apart. At this point, he also understands I come out ok on the other side of things, for the most part. But my black cloud is certainly entertaining for him. 'What could possibly happen to Aaron next and will I be there?'

Our conversation at Nana's Seafood was similar to many other conversations we've had over the years. Meaning, I probably didn't really interview him as much as I should have about the actual band. But now, getting towards the end of this book, I had more material and quotes than I needed. We talked about food. We talked shit about other bands. We talked shit about Emery band members. We talked shit about church. We talked shit about people in general. We talked a lot of shit.

But we also talked about not knowing what we are doing with our lives. We talked about our marriages and our kids. We talked about drinking, touring, and how huge As Cities Burn should have been. Licking our fingers of garlic sauce and figuring out how to eat a fucking crab, we just talked as friends. It wasn't an interview. Every other conversation for this book, although comfortable, felt like an interview. Even with Matt, who I am probably closest to from the band, it was an interview. I felt pressure to ask a good question, and drive the conversation in the right direction. By the time I got to Toby, I was just happy to hang out with a friend and eat seafood. So I'm not including a bunch of quotes from our conversation because it would be like just letting you listen in on any number of conversations I've had with Toby on the bus or at a bar; in the backroom of that House of Blues in San Diego when I felt that the whole world was coming down on me. You can go listen to Toby talk like crazy on his podcast. He never shuts the fuck up.

*****

I wanted to title this chapter, "TOBY: DIVA BITCH." I suppose it's not too late. Or, I could name it, "MY BEST FRIEND, TOBY". As I've mentioned, Toby is incredibly difficult to work for. He is demanding, emotional, unreasonable, irrational, insane, paranoid, gloomy, a bully, the list goes on... And yet, Toby is also one of the funniest mother fuckers I've ever known, and almost feels like a big brother, in some ways. But that's only good when you are just friends or peers with somebody. I had to *work* for him.

I've witnessed how difficult he can be with other tour managers. My favorite and oldest memory of Toby is at The Masquerade in Atlanta back in 2005. It was a sold out show, at the peak of "The Question" and Toby was...well, he was drunk. He was agro. The Masquerade is this really old historical landmark. We were all on the bus hanging out, and we see Toby outside kicking some sort of door or metal piece of something on the side of the building. I'm still not sure what it was. A security guy saw him and called the promoter and venue manager to tell him that the singer from Emery was "vandalizing" the venue. "Vandalizing" might be extreme, but nevertheless it was something for a tour manager to have to deal with. Cody Robinson, Emery's TM from Canada, was on the phone with the promoter. He was apologizing profusely, looking for Toby. Cody had that look in his eye. The look where the employee can't fucking believe he has to go ream out his boss.

"TOBY! GET YOUR ASS ON THE BUS! WHAT

THE FUCK ARE YOU DOING?"

Toby immediately goes into his double down mode that Matt talked about. "WHAT DID I DO? WHAT DID I DO?!"

Cody screams back, "Fucking vandalizing the venue that just took really good care of us, gave us extra liquor for free. Put on a kick ass show, and then you are gonna fuck their shit up!?"

"What door? I kicked a door? Oh my God. What did I do? They are mad about that? It was already broken!?"

Cody had started to leave the bus to continue to deal with the situation. Toby tried to follow, yelling, almost laughing, and trying to prove his innocence. "WHAT DID I DO?! WHAT DID I DO?!" he exclaimed over and over in his goofy Southern accent. The "DO" ramping up into a higher pitch each time.

"GET BACK ON THE BUS!" Cody yelled.

Toby was still trying to come down the steps as Cody was trying to shut the door, "WHAT DID I DO?!"

"GET BACK ON THE FUCKING BUS!" Cody screamed again, in his awesome Canadian "donchya know" accent where the "FUCKING" sounds like

"FUNKING".

This all goes on for a while. Cody avoids being fined by the venue and possibly even the City of Atlanta while Toby maintains his innocence to the very end.

My biggest confrontation with Toby was quite different and the circumstances less desirable. Emery had played a show at noon in Bakersfield, CA for some Reggae festival. It was just a totally stupid and awful show. So we made a rule that everyone had to drink a six pack of Bud Light before Emery went on stage. Now that made for a pretty fun morning. And it definitely made the show more fun. But now everyone was drunk and the day had a lot of time left in it. After the show, we collectively decided (emphasis on *collectively*) to drive to Santa Monica so we could hang out and longboard and wake up on the beach. Great idea, right?

I had my girlfriend, now wife, Cassie out on the road with us. This is not normal for a TM to have a significant other. But it was a pretty easy tour, with Hawkboy (my new project with Cody from ACB) opening for Emery . So the situation was unconventional. Also, Cassie had never met any of the Emery guys, or Cody, and I was in love with her. She is a terrific person, very nice and outgoing. I had started working for Emery only a couple months after my first marriage ended, so they had seen me go through the ringer. Then I had broken my leg…So, yeah, I was just seeking some redemption and maybe even a little bit of approval from my friends. "Hey guys! I know how to get a non-crazy person to fall in love with me! Should I marry her?"

Cassie was having a blast. She's amazing because I didn't feel the need to "babysit" her and make sure she was having a good time. She would sit down and talk to anyone, and I had all the space I needed to do my work everyday. It was great.

So on this day we are riding down to Santa Monica from Bakersfield just straight partying; drinking many more beers than the initial six. People broke out the Sharpies and started drawing on their faces while we rapped along to Dr. Dre and Eminem. It was everything you could love about touring with Emery. Dave got super fucked up and passed out before we ever made it to LA. The party started to die and Toby wanted to know the plan.

"Aaron, where are we gonna park?" Toby asked me.

"Ummm, I don't know. I guess we will have to get down there and scope it out." This was quite a normal procedure for touring in the Emery bus. This was the converted greyhound that we drove ourselves. Yes, if we were playing a show I would advance with the promoter to find out where the bus should park. But if we are just traveling to a town for a night off, we just go scope it out. Worst case scenario you end up at a Walmart.

"So hold up, we are just driving in Santa Monica…into LA and you don't even know where we are gonna take the bus?"

In response, I offered up a blank stare. I wasn't sure how to answer.

"This was your idea to go down there, and it's probably really hard to park, and you don't even know where to go. You are the TOUR MANAGER."

At this point, I'm feeling very uncomfortable. I'm on the front end of a reaming from my boss who is also my friend, in front of my girlfriend who I have only been with for about 6 months.

"TOURRRRR MANNNNAGERRR. It's your JOB."

"OK Toby. What do you want me to do?"

"YOURRR JOB. Where are we going to go? Are we trying to go to the beach? Find a park? How do you not know this? Tour Manager. You are the Tour Manager."

I love the memory I have of Matt's face throughout all of this. It's a smirk. Like, he knows this Toby so well. He knows that Toby cannot let this go right now. He doesn't totally agree with Toby, but he also isn't going to step in and take any blows for me. Matt wants no part of this conversation. It's very possible Matt also wanted a solution to the problem of parking. But he would have gone about it very differently; very reasonably without the humiliation.

"OK Toby, I'll see what I can do."

"THANK YOU. THANK YOU FOR DOING YOUR JOB."

I got on my phone for a while and did some searching. It was a ridiculous task. There is nowhere to read on the internet about, "Where to park a fucking bus in Santa Monica." I knew we would just cruise and find a parking lot. And if we didn't, we would just drive to a Walmart. But, I pretended to try and solve the problem.

I didn't hang out with the group for the rest of the

night. I was all rattled about it. I vented to Cassie and we went on a "date" down on the Santa Monica Peer. I couldn't stop fuming about it. But I bet you my best friend Toby was totally over it the minute we stepped off the bus. I could have hung out with him that night as if it had never happened. I don't know if that makes him a sociopath, or what. Maybe I don't know what a sociopath is.

The next day, everything was fine. Although Cassie did clean up a whole lot of puke that Dave spewed all over the aisle of the bus that night. I guess she earned her spot on the rig, as well as Toby's approval; a major accomplishment with the guy who thinks everyone is shitty. It was a successful tour, if you ask me.

Oh, also, I offered to pay Toby that $100 per diem out of my own pocket, but he didn't take it. That's how I know he wasn't actually so sure he didn't get it. If he thought I had really lost it, he would have taken that $100 from me in a second.

15

ARE YOU STILL LISTENING?

This book took about six months longer to write than I expected. I pitched it to BC Words as something I would have done by the end of January 2016. It's currently August 5, 2016 as I'm typing these words. Many factors played into this - procrastination, time management, being a full time student, lots of staring at the screen wondering what to write. I had no idea it would be so hard to write about my friends. And, my God, transcribing interviews is the worst. It's painfully boring. I had well over twenty hours of interviews to transcribe, which probably took sixty plus hours to sit and listen to and pull quotes from. Pausing and rewinding. Close listening trying to get the quotes right. Typing "ummmmmmmm" and "uhhhhhh" and "yeah" and "like." Where did we all learn to talk? Characters on "The West Wing" never say use these verbal these fillers. Maybe I should have had Aaron Sorkin write the script for these interviews.

My original outline for this book had a lot more to it than what I actually covered. It's amazing how much you can write about seemingly small topics. I never imagined that Josh's chapter would be the longest chapter of the book by many thousands of words. I wanted to do an entire chapter on crew members only - people that have worked for Emery over the years. Many of these people are just as interesting and fun to be around as the band members. They also served as an audience for guys like Matt and Toby to entertain. Their stories and experiences would be great for a book about "roadies". But I couldn't find a way to make it fit into this story.

Emery, the unlikely masters of rock. Matt should have been a doctor. Devin should have been a teacher; Toby, a country singer; Josh, a DJ; Dave, a loser that never left his hometown; Chopper, a bar musician in Nashville. And, Seth…well, I think Seth actually ended up doing what he should be doing, working as a counselor. He got out early with his soul still intact. He wasn't in long enough for the entertainment industry to stunt his maturity into adulthood.

For everything that these guys should have been, they chose to do what they wanted. They carved their own path, however unlikely the chances of success may have been. They went against family to take a major risk. Emery learned how to survive. They learned how to look cool. They learned how to run a business. They learned how to apply their musical influences to create something that connected with hundreds of thousands of people. When I first heard Emery, I thought there was no way they would get as big as they got. This band got big, y'all. Selling almost two-hundred-thousand is no small feat. In the major label world, that would have been an incredible disappointment. But in our world, they launched themselves into the top one percent of artists. At that level, major labels do start to take interest. After the success of "The Question", Emery was under contract for one more record with Tooth and Nail. Everyone expected that third and final Tooth and Nail record to be a big hit. There was no reason to think that the record that would eventually be named "I'm Only a Man" wouldn't only further build off the success of "The Question". Brandon Ebel tried to sign Emery to a new contract before IOAM came out. He offered Emery somewhere in the neighborhood of half a million dollars to re-sign. They turned it down.

Emery had a big time manager and that big time manager was talking to big time label people. Hawthorne Heights – peers and tour mates of Emery – had just signed something like a million dollar contract with a major. Emery expected IOAM to sell well enough to garner a similar contract. Why would you take $450,000 when you were almost certain you could get $1,000,000?

IOAM "flopped". It sold less than "The Question" sold first week and never caught steam. The music on IOAM was only a slight departure from "The Question", but it was enough to essentially cut their fan base in half. The first single "The Party Song" was not well received, and I think that was enough to stifle the excitement of the fan base leading up to the release. They took some artistic liberties on that record. I sensed a bit of invincibility coming from them. How could they go wrong? They were big and beloved by so many.

All Emery had to do was write "The Question" Pt. 2. Eventually they did. "In Shallow Seas We Sail" comes off as a more appropriate follow up to "The Question". If they had put out that record instead of IOAM, I think they would have gotten their million-dollar deal. Instead, Emery hired a big shot manager who took them in a direction that basically abandoned what they were good at and abandoned the very people they were selling music to. He was going to make them a "real" big band. That manager took over all communication between the band and the label. Emery had gone pro, but it didn't work out. After IOAM flopped, Emery resigned with Tooth and Nail. But the $450,000 offer was gone; way gone. Emery, the unlikely masters of rock, were officially on the downslope of their career.

"Masters of rock." I didn't pull that out of thin air. When I started tour managing the band, I became responsible for holding on to the band credit card. (Side note: I failed miserably at that task once when I let it fly out the window while I was driving the bus.) I took the card from Matt and looked at it. On the card where the business name is printed, it read: "Emery The Masters of Rock LLC". That was the official name of the business that is Emery in the eyes of financial institutions and the law. So every time I went to settle up with the promoter after as show, I had to inform them to write out the check to "Emery The Masters of Rock LLC". Every time I had to fill out a W-2, under business name I had to write "Emery The Masters of Rock LLC".

"Is this a power play?" I remember thinking. Yes, it's funny and mostly in jest. But, if you say something enough you begin to believe it, right? It did influence the name of this book. And while "The Masters of Rock" – unlikely or not – might be a bit over the top in describing Emery and their career, I will tell you that they most definitely think highly of themselves as a band. Compared to many other artists I have known, they seem to struggle less with the insecurities that typically come with the territory. Matt is so pragmatic and unaffected in an emotional sense by criticism that he can laser focus and just do the work. To me, that is the biggest problem many artists face when it comes to their creation. They focus way too much on the art, and not enough on the work aspect. I'm not suggesting that we should dilute art to simply a commercial product. I'm saying sometimes you just need to get the fuck over yourself and do the work. That doesn't mean that everything you do in that structure will be gold. But eventually the art you desire will poke its head through. I remember reading about Ben Gibbard, the singer for Death Cab for Cutie (another Seattle band mind you...so basically in Emery's "local" scene) saying that he got an "office" in downtown Seattle that he made into a writing studio. He would go there everyday like a job from nine to five, or whatever, and work. The idea that not every minute of every day spent creating art is going to be life changing is a healthy approach. Emery excels at this. Even Toby, easily the most emotional of the bunch, knows how to buckle down and do work. Emery is his *job*. Emery can't afford to be at the mercy of his insecurities and artistic whims. There is a job to do and that job is to write songs, make records, and entertain people.

You think Emery likes playing shows these days? It's the worst part of the day on tour, save Josh. Toby is forty years old. Hell, I'm thirty-three and playing a show is the worst part of the day on tour. It's the work. But

Toby drags his ass up there every night and gets it done. He does the work.

Most bands at this point in their career would have broken up a long time ago. Bands go so hard for so long and then when they hit that downslope they think it's all over. Underoath is a great example of a band that kicked ass, and then out of nowhere kids stopped coming to the shows by the thousands. Oversaturation? Maybe. Loss of interest by fans? Possibly. Decrease in quality of the art? Doubtful, although I don't know, because I was never an Underoath fan. I don't know what caused the decline specifically, but I do know that when it happened, that band had the all or nothing mentality. If we can't be UNDEROATH we just won't be. So they did a farewell tour. They didn't need to break up. They just needed a break. They needed to lower the supply and increase the demand. And they needed to lower their expectations for what their band *had* to be going forward; not artistically, just logistically. I truly believe that every band that comes down from the peak of success should follow the Emery business model. Figure out how much time key members can put into the band. Cater to those key members. Figure out how to be more independent. What good is a label when a band can go out and get $200K from a crowdfund? There is more artistic and career freedom in 2016 for artists than in the entire history of the modern music industry. Just go off the grid of the music "industry". Make your own way. Be like Emery.

In 2016, Matt didn't want to play normal shows. So they came up with the plan to do all acoustic VIP-type show experiences. The price is higher than a normal show with less in attendance. It's working. They are generating significant revenue on their own terms. The band is happy with the format. It's something different. It's fresh. It's less exhausting than flailing around on stage for sixty minutes; chillin' on a stool and jamming some chill ass screamo songs. It's even allowed Devin to practically return to the band as a full member after leaving several years back.

Emery has also diversified their revenue streams. Matt and Toby are at the forefront of this because of their involvement with BadChristian and all the different projects attached to it - podcasts, music promotion and distribution, book publishing, fan club memberships, and much more to come in the future. Devin launched a successful crowdfund for a solo project. Matt has other business endeavors totally separate from BadChristian. Toby just quit his church job in Charleston to move to Nashville and pursue songwriting, more podcasting, and entertainment in general. And they have done all these things using Emery as a springboard. It makes sense. If you have a large group of people that have cared enough to give you money in exchange for music, maybe they will be interested in some other stuff you have going on. You don't think if Underoath wanted to they could launch a similar organization? Personalities play into that theory and I'm not suggesting a podcast is the way to go like it was with Matt and Toby. But I am saying Underoath could do anything they wanted to do if they would just utilize their audience the way that Emery has. The same goes for every band out there that is refusing to adapt their business and take advantage of what they call a "captive audience". Maybe this book should have been titled, "Emery: The Masters of Diversifying their Screamo Band's Revenue Streams".

*****

Over the years, anytime anybody has ever asked me who's my favorite band to tour with, the answer has always been, "Oh, definitely Emery. Hands down." For years I was naïve enough to think that surely As Cities Burn was their favorite too. I mean, we had so much fun on their tours! We were tour besties. I either read an interview, or maybe heard the guys giving an interview while I was their tour manager, and the question to Emery was, "Who has been your favorite band to tour with?" In my head I was like, "Here it comes. The As Cities Burn shout out." I don't have the direct quotes, but, they basically said their favorite bands to tour with were Dropkick Murphy's and Boy's Night Out.

Nair a mention of my band. This is fine, though. I'll tell you what it is about Emery that makes them so fun to tour with. Once you are in with them – kind of welcomed into their inner circle of tour hangs – it's such a good time that you are blinded by the fact that they are entertaining the hell out of you, giving the illusion that you must be entertaining the hell out of them. You ain't. This doesn't bum me out. If anything it makes me want to find a way to get on tour with Dropkick Murphy's and Boy's Night Out ASAP!

Even though I regret signing up to write this book in some ways, the reason I did it was because of how interesting a group of guys Emery is. "A band is from a small town and they move and get a record deal and find success." It's barely a synopsis, and it's one that isn't too interesting on the surface. I hope I made you understand why this group of guys is special and worthy of writing about. I hope that the unlikeliness of this band is not simply confined to the aforementioned boring synopsis. The unlikeliness did not end at "got a record deal, sold records, man those guys talk funny, isn't that weird that those goofballs got big?" The unlikeliness of Emery continues to permeate on a daily basis, as evidenced by the fact that they are still going. This may seriously be a 'until death do us part' situation. And I'm not entirely sure that if Toby died, Matt wouldn't find some way to crowdfund a "Toby is Dead" record and do a tour using holograms. I would bet all the money in my pocket against all the money in your pocket (if you noticed that I lifted this from Aaron Sorkin's greatest character, Toby Ziegler, then kudos to you; otherwise, I will retain credit for the phrase) that Emery will never write the Facebook post that so many other bands have to make – a farewell tour announcement.

They've come too far – all the way from obscurity in a shit southern town to a surprisingly stabilized and profitable career – to throw in the towel because of the idea that it's goofy for a forty-year-old man to sing and scream the opening to "Walls". In 2004, Toby screamed with authority the question that would launch a life-changing journey. "Are You Listening?" The fact that you have read this book is proof that you are *still* listening.

Emery – the masters – will play on.

Made in the USA
Middletown, DE
20 September 2018